The History of Love

CRAFTED BY SKRIUWER

Copyright © 2025 by Skriuwer.

All rights reserved. No part of this book may be used or reproduced in any form whatsoever without written permission except in the case of brief quotations in critical articles or reviews.

At **Skriuwer**, we're more than just a team—we're a global community of people who love books. In Frisian, "Skriuwer" means "writer," and that's at the heart of what we do: creating and sharing books with readers worldwide. Wherever you are in the world, **Skriuwer** is here to inspire learning.

Frisian is one of the oldest languages in Europe, closely related to English and Dutch, and is spoken by about **500,000 people** in the province of **Friesland** (Fryslân), located in the northern Netherlands. It's the second official language of the Netherlands, but like many minority languages, Frisian faces the challenge of survival in a modern, globalized world.

We're using the money we earn to promote the Frisian language. For more information, contact : **kontakt@skriuwer.com** (www.skriuwer.com)

For more information, contact : **kontakt@skriuwer.com** (www.skriuwer.com)

TABLE OF CONTENTS

CHAPTER 1: LOVE IN PREHISTORIC TIMES

- *Survival and pair bonding among early humans*
- *Communal responsibilities shaping relationships*
- *Evidence from prehistoric art and burial practices*
- *Importance of child-rearing and group dynamics*

CHAPTER 2: LOVE IN ANCIENT MESOPOTAMIA

- *Marriage contracts and legal frameworks*
- *Influence of deities like Inanna/Ishtar on love*
- *Economic and social dimensions of relationships*
- *Early examples of romantic poetry and letters*

CHAPTER 3: LOVE IN ANCIENT EGYPT

- *Family structure and strong marital bonds*
- *Divine models of love (Isis and Osiris)*
- *Emphasis on the afterlife and eternal devotion*
- *Love poetry and daily expressions of affection*

CHAPTER 4: LOVE IN BIBLICAL TIMES

- *Patriarchal family structures and covenant themes*
- *Marriage as a social and sacred bond*
- *Polygamy, concubinage, and associated tensions*
- *Song of Songs as a celebration of romantic love*

CHAPTER 5: LOVE IN ANCIENT GREECE

- *Different Greek words for love (Eros, Philia, Agape)*
- *Philosophical explorations (Plato, Aristotle) on love*
- *Myths and their impact on cultural perceptions*
- *Role of city-states and social norms in relationships*

CHAPTER 6: LOVE IN THE HELLENISTIC WORLD

- *Cultural blending post-Alexander's conquests*
- *Spread of Greek ideas about relationships*
- *Influence of mystery cults and syncretism*
- *New family structures and personal freedoms*

CHAPTER 7: LOVE IN ANCIENT ROME

- *Marriage as a legal and political institution*
- *Romantic literature and the art of seduction (Ovid)*
- *Social class influencing marital choices*
- *Changing family laws under the Empire*

CHAPTER 8: LOVE IN EARLY CHRISTIANITY

- *Teachings on spiritual love and compassion*
- *Marriage as both sacred covenant and communal duty*
- *Celibacy and religious devotion shaping relationships*
- *Emergence of Christian ethics affecting family life*

CHAPTER 9: LOVE IN THE ISLAMIC GOLDEN AGE

- Poetic traditions celebrating romantic and divine love
- Influence of Islamic law on marriage and family
- Philosophical and theological perspectives on affection
- Cultural exchange across diverse regions

CHAPTER 10: LOVE IN MEDIEVAL EUROPE

- Feudal structures and arranged marriages
- Role of the Church in defining marital rules
- Honor, lineage, and family alliances
- Daily life and emotional ties within the household

CHAPTER 11: COURTLY LOVE IN THE HIGH MIDDLE AGES

- Chivalry and romantic ideals guiding noble behavior
- Literary influences (knights, ladies, devotion)
- Social etiquette in royal and noble courts
- Shift from feudal obligations to personal longing

CHAPTER 12: TROUBADOURS, MINNESINGERS, AND POETIC LOVE

- Rise of lyrical expressions of romance in song
- Regional traditions in France and Germany
- Traveling minstrels shaping cultural views on love
- Influence on European poetry and music

CHAPTER 13: LOVE IN THE RENAISSANCE

- Humanism and renewed focus on individual emotion
- Art, literature, and new modes of desire
- Blending religious devotion with worldly affection
- Patronage systems and courtly intrigue

CHAPTER 14: LOVE AND THE REFORMATION

- Changes in marriage laws under Protestant influences
- Catholic responses and continued traditions
- Family piety and evolving moral codes
- Social impact of religious upheaval on relationships

CHAPTER 15: LOVE IN THE EARLY MODERN PERIOD

- Growth of nation-states and shifts in family structure
- Cultural exchanges through exploration and trade
- Personal diaries and correspondence revealing intimacy
- Changing norms of courtship and spousal roles

CHAPTER 16: THE BAROQUE ERA AND LOVE

- Dramatic emotional expressions in art and music
- Influence of absolute monarchies on marriage alliances
- Religious tensions shaping personal devotion
- Lavish displays of affection in courtly life

CHAPTER 17: THE ENLIGHTENMENT AND CHANGING VIEWS ON LOVE

- *Emphasis on reason and individual rights*
- *Philosophical debates on marriage and personal freedom*
- *Emergence of the companionate marriage ideal*
- *Continued influence of emotional depth despite rational focus*

CHAPTER 18: THE ROMANTIC MOVEMENT AND LOVE

- *Reaction against Enlightenment rationality*
- *Celebration of intense emotion and personal expression*
- *Rise of romantic literature and poetry*
- *Impact on courtship practices and gender roles*

CHAPTER 19: THE VICTORIAN AGE AND LOVE

- *Strict social codes and hidden passions*
- *Marriage as both a moral and economic institution*
- *Idealization of domestic life and family unity*
- *Literary reflections on restrained yet powerful affection*

CHAPTER 20: EARLY 20TH CENTURY PERSPECTIVES ON LOVE

- *Lingering traditions versus emerging social changes*
- *Influence of industrialization on family dynamics*
- *Burgeoning interest in psychology and human emotion*
- *Transitional views on romance before modernity fully unfolds*

CHAPTER 1

Love in Prehistoric Times

Prehistoric times cover a massive span of human existence. Although we do not have written records from that era, archaeological findings, anthropological research, and comparisons with existing hunter-gatherer societies help us form an understanding of how early humans might have experienced love, attachment, and family bonds. During this long stretch of time, people dealt with basic survival needs like finding food, shelter, and security from predators or rival groups. These challenges shaped the forms of relationships and social rules that likely guided early love and partnership.

In order to explore love in prehistoric times, we need to imagine a world without writing, organized states, or modern conveniences. Early humans lived in small kin-based groups. They hunted, gathered wild plants, and moved across the land in search of resources. Because of these conditions, close cooperation was a matter of life and death. Sharing food, caring for children, and defending the group from dangers were all group efforts. For these reasons, the idea of pairing up as partners or forming stable families might have been linked to survival and communal ties.

The Role of Pair Bonding in Human Evolution

Anthropologists have long debated how pair bonding—long-term relationships between adults—became a feature of human life. Many believe that human infants are born more helpless compared to those of other animals. They need constant care for many years before they can fend for themselves. This led to a social structure where two caregivers could split responsibilities, allowing one to find food while the other protected the child or children. Over time, this pattern might have formed the basis of long-term attachments between adults.

These attachments go beyond simple mating. They include emotional bonds and affection. While we cannot step back in time to see exactly how prehistoric people felt, we can guess that caring feelings were critical for a stable relationship. If emotional closeness made parents less likely to split up or less likely to neglect children, those traits might have been favored over generations. Certain hormone-driven feelings—like those we today call "love" or "attachment"—likely played a big part in bonding.

Courtship and Mating Rituals

Even though we do not have direct evidence of prehistoric "courtship," we can consider how many existing small-scale societies or tribal groups handle courtship and marriage. Often, families or the small group have a say in who pairs with whom. This is done to ensure alliances or share labor. Though it might differ from our modern romantic ideals, it still reflects a kind of love or at least a form of mutual dependency. There might have been rituals to show interest, such as gift-giving, dancing, or shared tasks like hunting or gathering.

In some tribal societies that continue to exist around the world, couples come together during communal events, like dances or festivals, where youths showcase their abilities. If any parallels existed in prehistoric times, then love or partnership might have been expressed through demonstrations of skill, generosity, or willingness to cooperate. While we cannot be certain, we can assume that showing one's ability to hunt or gather could have been just as important as personal affection.

The Importance of Kinship

Family ties in prehistoric communities often extended beyond the couple and their children. Grandparents, siblings, cousins, and other relatives likely lived close together. Love for one's family might have had a different focus than modern ideas of the nuclear family. The entire group offered mutual support and protection. Because survival often depended on many hands working together, the kind of love that existed within these groups extended to caring for each other's children, sharing food, and protecting the group from external threats.

One crucial aspect was that the sense of "love" would have been intertwined with a sense of group loyalty. If the group worked as a team, people would feel attached not only to a partner but also to their extended family. This attachment was likely very strong because group safety and well-being were essential. In such a setting, the line between romantic love, familial love, and communal responsibility might have been blurred.

Rituals and Symbolic Expressions

Although we lack detailed records from prehistoric times, early art might hold clues to how people expressed affection. Cave paintings from sites like Lascaux in France or Altamira in Spain often depict animals and hunts, but there are also handprints and symbols. Some scholars suggest that certain shapes might have been symbolic of fertility or life. Figurines such as the "Venus" statues (for instance, the Venus of Willendorf) seem to emphasize fertility and the female form. These artifacts might hint at a prehistoric appreciation for female fertility, motherhood, and possibly the nurturing aspect of love.

Rites of passage were also part of prehistoric societies, marking stages from childhood to adulthood. During these rites, it is possible that early humans recognized the bond between mates or the responsibilities of parenthood. While we do not know the exact nature of these ceremonies, it is likely that prehistoric people had a strong sense of continuity between generations, celebrating fertility, birth, and the raising of children.

Gender Roles and Their Impact on Love

In many hunter-gatherer groups, tasks are divided along gender lines: men often take part in hunting, and women often focus on gathering, child-rearing, and domestic tasks. But this division was not always strict. Early humans might have developed flexible roles to deal with changing environments. That said, certain general patterns might have shaped how love developed.

Men who could hunt successfully might have been seen as attractive partners because they brought in needed resources. Women who were skilled at gathering or had strong nurturing abilities were likely seen as valuable too. Love, in this sense, might have included an element of respect for what each partner contributed. This mutual dependence would foster emotional bonds. Over time, these bonds might have turned into lifelong attachments that contributed to stable family units.

In groups where resources were scarce, there might have been competition for the most capable or socially valuable partners. At the same time, cooperation was key to survival, so a partner's willingness to share and care for the group could be as important as physical strength or skill. In these circumstances, people learned how to show positive qualities that made them good partners in the eyes of the group. This practical approach to love does not cancel out emotional connection. In fact, the daily struggle to survive could have deepened feelings of closeness and dependence.

Parenting and Love for Children

Parent-child relationships in prehistoric times were shaped by high infant mortality rates, dangers in the environment, and the need for constant care. Still, the universal bond between parent and child likely existed then as it does now. Mothers, fathers, grandparents, and siblings might have cooperated in child-rearing. With more caretakers, the child's chance of survival increased.

This communal approach to child-rearing might have also influenced how love was expressed. Children were seen as a communal resource for the future. This means that the love for a child was not just the concern of the parents but of the entire group. As a result, early humans likely developed strong empathy and protective instincts for all young ones. In many ways, the survival of the tribe depended on healthy new generations, so love and concern for children was widespread.

Social Bonds and Conflicts

Prehistoric love did not exist in a vacuum of pure harmony. Small communities had their share of conflicts. Rivalries over mates, disputes over resources, and external threats from other groups could cause friction. In such an environment, the way love was understood might include a sense of loyalty and duty, not just individual desire. Jealousy or competition over partners could lead to tension within the group, so it was in everyone's best interest to keep some balance or follow unwritten rules.

Conflicts might have also driven people to form alliances through pair bonding. A union between members of different groups could be a way to settle disputes or create ties that benefited the community. In this sense, love or marriage in prehistoric times was also political, helping to strengthen networks and reduce hostilities. While personal feelings were important, practical needs often guided how relationships formed and lasted.

The Evolution of Emotional Expression

Humans communicate emotion through facial expressions, body language, and vocalization. Long before spoken language became complex, people likely used touch, eye contact, and tone of voice to convey care or affection. As language developed, so did the capacity to speak about feelings, even if only in simple terms. This would have allowed deeper expressions of love, bonding, and devotion. An affectionate gesture, a comforting touch, or shared laughter all helped forge emotional ties.

Songs and rhythmic activities, like clapping or drumming, might have played a role too. Music can bring people together and create shared emotional experiences. If prehistoric communities had any form of group singing or chanting, it might have strengthened the sense of belonging and unity. Over time, these communal expressions of emotion became part of cultural traditions, possibly paving the way for more formal rituals about love and partnership.

Symbolic Artifacts and Personal Ornaments

Archaeological findings suggest that early humans created personal ornaments such as necklaces, bracelets, or carved items out of bone, shell, or stone. These decorations could have had symbolic meanings. Some might have served as status markers or protective talismans, while others might have been tokens exchanged between mates or family members, representing unity or affection.

A simple shell necklace could have said many things: it might have showed that the wearer belonged to a certain group, that they had a special connection to another person, or that they had achieved some level of respect within the tribe. When placed in the context of love, such an ornament might have been given as a gift to show care or commitment. We see in modern times that jewelry is often connected to love and marriage, so it is not far-fetched to think a simpler version existed in the distant past.

Death Burial, and Expressions of Love

One of the strongest indicators that prehistoric people had deep emotional attachments is how they buried their dead. Archaeologists have found graves containing tools, ornaments, and other goods, which may suggest a belief in an afterlife or, at least, a desire to honor the departed. The inclusion of personal items in a grave can be interpreted as a sign of affection, respect, or sorrow. Burials were not just about disposing of a body; they were social or spiritual events that might have given survivors a chance to express love for the deceased.

In some prehistoric burial sites, people were found to be placed in specific positions, or wrapped with care, sometimes alongside tokens or even the remains of animals. These actions show that the living paid special attention to their loved ones, giving them items for the journey after death or simply displaying their respect. Such practices highlight the emotional depth and the communal sense of love, as well as the importance of memory and legacy.

Shifts Over Time

Because "prehistoric" covers a large time frame, we should note that forms of love and bonding would have changed as human societies advanced. When humans began to farm and settle in one place (the Neolithic Revolution), social structures started to shift. Property and land became important, and the idea of inheritance might have added new layers to partnership and family. This shift toward settled communities and domestication of animals changed the daily roles of men, women, and children, and might have influenced how love and marriage were viewed.

However, for most of prehistory, humans lived in a world of hunting and gathering. This lifestyle fostered mobile, flexible groupings. Although we can only speculate, we can guess that love in these communities was a powerful, bonding force that made cooperation possible. Emotional ties would have been woven into every aspect of life—food sharing, child-rearing, group defense, and more.

Understanding Prehistoric Love Through Modern Tribes

Studying modern hunter-gatherer or tribal societies can provide small windows into the past. While no modern group is exactly like a Stone Age community, certain behaviors can offer clues. Many tribal groups place a high value on communal sharing and collective responsibility. Love, therefore, is often expressed not only as romantic attachment between two adults but also as a sense of care for the larger group. There is less focus on individual ownership and more on what benefits everyone.

In many such groups, marriage can be more of an agreement between families than a purely private romance. Yet, that does not mean there is no genuine affection. Couples can still form strong emotional bonds. The group context only shapes how and when people can express or formalize that bond. If something similar applied in prehistoric times, we can see that love was always part of a bigger social framework. It was a feeling between individuals, but also a resource for the group.

The Emotional Core of Early Human Life

Ultimately, love in prehistoric times might have been both simple and profound. Simple, because it was closely tied to daily survival and basic emotional needs; profound, because it was essential for forming stable bonds and ensuring group cohesion. Parents and children relied on each other, mates relied on each other, and individuals relied on their community. In turn, the entire group relied on close, trusting relationships to thrive and avoid extinction.

Though we cannot read prehistoric love poems or diaries, we can guess that strong emotions existed based on what we know about human biology and behavior. The capacity to feel empathy, to attach emotionally, and to long for the closeness of others is part of what makes us human. This capacity did not just appear in recorded history; it must have been present long before people wrote about it.

CHAPTER 2

Love in Ancient Mesopotamia

Ancient Mesopotamia, often called the "Cradle of Civilization," refers to the region between the Tigris and Euphrates Rivers (modern-day Iraq and parts of neighboring countries). This area saw the rise of some of the earliest known human civilizations, such as Sumer, Akkad, Babylon, and Assyria. Because these societies developed writing systems (like cuneiform), we have some of the world's oldest written records. These include myths, laws, letters, and economic documents that shed light on how people in this region understood love, marriage, and family.

The Importance of Written Records

Mesopotamian civilizations invented cuneiform around the end of the 4th millennium BCE. This system involved pressing a reed stylus into clay tablets, creating wedge-shaped marks. Among the earliest writings we have are economic lists and administrative records, but soon, scribes began writing myths, poetry, and legal codes. These documents let us see aspects of daily life, including personal relationships.

The famous **Epic of Gilgamesh**, often cited as the oldest epic poem, touches on themes of friendship and human emotion. While it is not a love story in the romantic sense, it does illustrate the importance of close bonds. It also shows how the Mesopotamians viewed their gods as deeply involved in human affairs, including relationships. Other myths, such as the story of **Inanna (or Ishtar)**—the goddess of love and war—reveal how the Mesopotamians connected the power of love with the forces of nature and life itself.

The Concept of Love in Mesopotamia

For Mesopotamians, love was not a purely private emotion. It was also a social, legal, and religious affair. People got married, raised families, and formed alliances as part of a larger social structure. At the same time, many myths portray the gods themselves experiencing passion, jealousy, and desire. The goddess Inanna/Ishtar is often shown as a figure who can grant love or wreak havoc when spurned. Thus, love was both divine and human, associated with fertility, power, and sometimes conflict.

Although we should not equate ancient Mesopotamian love directly with modern love, there are familiar elements. For instance, letters between spouses have been discovered, showing affection and concern for each other's well-being. Some messages discuss daily worries, while others express longing for a partner's presence. These sources tell us that individuals cared for each other in ways that were both practical and emotional.

Marriage Contracts and Family Structure

One of the strongest pieces of evidence about love and marriage comes from the many clay tablets that served as marriage contracts or property documents. These contracts usually listed the terms of marriage, such as dowries, bride prices, and inheritance rights. Marriage was often a family arrangement involving negotiations between the two families. The groom's family might give goods or money to the bride's family in exchange for her hand in marriage. Meanwhile, the bride might bring a dowry into the marriage, including household items or land.

Even if these contracts might seem transactional, that does not mean love was absent. Instead, it shows that marriage also had economic and social dimensions. Families wanted to ensure that any union would be beneficial and stable. Once married, the couple usually lived together in the husband's family home, though exceptions existed. The extended family played a key role, with elders guiding many decisions.

Romantic Poetry and Mythology

Love in Mesopotamia was also reflected in poems and myths. We see references to the intimacy between gods and goddesses, sometimes described in vivid detail. For example, certain hymns dedicated to Inanna and Dumuzi (her consort) talk about their sacred marriage, symbolizing fertility of the land and the prosperity of the people. These hymns can be quite passionate, describing embraces, kisses, and longing. Although the language can be symbolic—representing crops growing or the renewal of life—it also serves as an early example of how deeply love was woven into cultural narratives.

Some poems speak of physical attraction, describing the beloved's beauty in simple but heartfelt terms. While these might be addressed to gods, they also give us an idea of how humans at the time might have understood desire and pleasure. The very existence of such poetry suggests that people valued romantic feelings and recognized the emotional power behind them.

Roles of Men and Women

In ancient Mesopotamia, men typically held most positions of power, both in the family and society. However, women could own property, run businesses, and even become priestesses. The laws and customs varied by city-state and time period, but overall, there was a structured approach to family life. Wives were expected to manage the household, bear children, and maintain family honor. Husbands were expected to provide for and protect the family.

In many legal codes, there were rules about adultery, divorce, and the rights of children. For example, **The Code of Hammurabi** (circa 18th century BCE) outlines specific punishments for those who break marital vows. Such laws show that love, or at least marital fidelity and social order, was taken seriously. At the same time, men could have concubines, and polygamy was allowed in some circumstances, often tied to the need for heirs. This structure could create tension within families, but it was also widely accepted as part of the social system.

Expressions of Affection in Daily Life

Although we have many official documents, we also have personal letters and records that reveal how Mesopotamians cared for one another. For instance, letters show wives asking husbands to bring certain goods home, or expressing worry over their health. Husbands sometimes wrote back affectionately, calling their wives by endearing names. These small details highlight that, behind the grand structures of temples and palaces, ordinary people experienced tender moments of connection.

People might exchange small gifts. Jewelry was popular, as were seals—stone or clay cylinders carved with images or writing that could be rolled onto wet clay to leave an impression. A personal seal might be a sign of identity and status, but it could also be an intimate token. A husband might give a new seal to his wife to mark her place in the family business. Alternatively, a wife might craft or decorate something to personalize her husband's possessions, showing care through craftsmanship.

The Role of Religion in Love and Marriage

Religion pervaded every part of life in Mesopotamia. Each city had a patron deity, and people would pray for protection, success in business, good harvests, and family well-being. When it came to love, people might ask the gods for a suitable spouse or for help with fertility. Certain rituals were performed to honor love and fertility deities, asking them to bless the union and offspring. Temple complexes sometimes played a role in the arrangement of marriages, especially if one or both partners held a religious position.

The concept of the "sacred marriage" appears in several Mesopotamian myths, most notably those involving Inanna and Dumuzi. In these stories, the union of the goddess and her consort represents the cyclical nature of the seasons—life, death, and rebirth. Ritual enactments of these myths might have occurred in temples, sometimes involving the king and a priestess as symbolic stand-ins for the deities. This shows how love, in the form of divine union, was linked to fertility and abundance for the entire community.

Conflict and Jealousy in Mesopotamian Texts

Because Mesopotamia was home to many city-states and dynasties, conflicts were common—wars, rivalries, and power struggles shaped politics and family alliances. This context influenced personal relationships, too. Marriage could be used to build ties between powerful families or to seal treaties between city-states. On a personal level, jealousy and betrayal are themes in some Mesopotamian myths. The goddess Inanna/Ishtar, for instance, could be wrathful when crossed. This divine reflection of jealousy suggests that ordinary people also experienced such emotions.

In daily life, if a spouse felt wronged or suspected unfaithfulness, the matter could be brought before elders or temple officials for judgment. The code-based legal system spelled out the consequences, which could be harsh. At the same time, the existence of these laws means that emotional turmoil and disputes were recognized parts of life, needing structured solutions. This balance between strong emotion and regulated social norms is a recurring theme in the ancient world.

Fertility and Family Legacy

Family continuity was of great importance. Having children was not only about personal joy but also about ensuring the family line and securing labor for the household. Many Mesopotamian couples prayed to gods for children, made offerings, and followed rituals believed to increase fertility. If a couple could not have a child, it could lead to social and emotional stress. Sometimes surrogacy or adoption was considered, though the laws around these practices varied.

Love for children is evident in texts discussing inheritance and family care. Parents showed concern for their offspring's future and sometimes set aside property for them. There are also references to the emotional bond between parents and children in letters and personal communications. Archaeological sites reveal children's toys, indicating that beyond the practical aim of raising heirs, there was likely genuine affection and a desire to nurture the younger generation.

Social Status and Its Effect on Love

Class played a large role in ancient Mesopotamia. Society was broadly divided into nobility, free commoners, and slaves. Marriages typically occurred within the same social strata, though exceptions existed. A nobleman might take a concubine from a lower status, but such a relationship held different rights and obligations than a formal marriage to a noblewoman. Love across class lines, if it existed, faced practical and social barriers.

Still, we have stories and myths where a deity or royal figure falls for someone of lower status, showing that the idea of love crossing boundaries existed, at least in literature. Ordinary people of similar status likely had more freedom to form attachments based on mutual affection, though family and economic considerations always loomed large.

Literary Works Reflecting Love

Apart from mythological texts, Sumerian and Akkadian poetry sometimes explored human emotions in direct ways. Scholars have found poems celebrating the beauty of a beloved or the joy of physical union. Although these works are fragmented, they provide glimpses into how Mesopotamians could express personal longing and delight. This stands as an early example of love poetry that connects us with the deep emotional life of people who lived thousands of years ago.

One of the well-known sets of texts are the so-called "Temple Hymns" and "Sacred Marriage" poems, which include lines that compare the beloved's body to fragrant plants or sweet honey. Even though these might be part of religious ceremonies, they contain genuine-sounding references to desire and tenderness. This overlap of religious devotion and personal affection underscores the integral role love played in their worldview.

Divorce and Separation

While marriage was often a permanent arrangement, divorce did happen in ancient Mesopotamia. The legal codes allowed for it under certain conditions, such as infertility or serious misconduct. A husband could divorce his wife, but he had to return her dowry. In some laws, if the wife was at fault, she might lose part of her dowry or face a harsher penalty. These regulations tried to balance property rights and the social need for stability. The fact that divorce was an option suggests that not all unions were based solely on love or that love could end, prompting legal remedies.

Parent-Child Letters and Emotional Closeness

We also have examples of letters between parents and children, which can be very tender. In these letters, a father might scold a son for neglecting his duties but still express concern for his health and well-being. A mother might urge a daughter to be careful with her husband's family and remind her that she is loved. These personal accounts show that family members cared about each other's emotional state and practical needs. Love was not just a fleeting passion between spouses; it was also the bond that held families together.

Love Beyond Death

Like their prehistoric ancestors, Mesopotamians placed importance on how they treated their dead. They practiced burial in family tombs or communal cemeteries, leaving grave goods for the afterlife. This practice suggests that people believed the dead continued to exist in some form. Ancestors could be honored with offerings to keep them content in the underworld. Love for deceased relatives was shown through rituals, prayers, and the maintenance of burial sites. This sense of ongoing duty and affection might also have mirrored how love was never just for the present but carried responsibilities over time.

Influence on Later Civilizations

Ancient Mesopotamia's ideas about love, marriage, and family influenced neighboring regions and later empires. Their laws, myths, and literature inspired or shaped cultures in the broader Near East, including those of the Hebrews, Hittites, and later the Persians. Some of their stories and legal frameworks found echoes in biblical texts and in the oral traditions that spread across the ancient world. This means that Mesopotamian perspectives on love set patterns that persisted for centuries.

CHAPTER 3

LOVE IN ANCIENT EGYPT

Ancient Egypt was one of the most enduring civilizations in world history, lasting for thousands of years along the fertile banks of the Nile River. During this time, the Egyptians developed unique traditions regarding love, marriage, and family life. The cultural and religious ideas of Egypt guided how people saw relationships, personal commitment, and even the afterlife. In this chapter, we will explore the various aspects of love in Ancient Egypt, including family structure, marriage rules, expressions of affection, myths about divine love, and how people carried their devotion beyond death.

The Importance of the Nile and Daily Life

The Nile River played a vital role in shaping Ancient Egyptian society. Its regular flooding brought rich soil that produced abundant crops. Because food resources were reliable most of the time, families could focus on building a structured society. Egyptians lived in villages and towns spread along the river, with a few major cities like Memphis and Thebes. In these communities, most people worked as farmers, laborers, or craftsmen, while scribes and officials managed the government.

When it came to love, the stable environment allowed Egyptians to form bonds that were not only practical but also emotional. Families worked together in the fields, shared resources, and passed property down through generations. Though survival remained a concern, the relative stability provided people with the chance to invest more emotional energy in personal relationships.

Religious Beliefs and Love

Religion touched every part of Egyptian life, including how people understood love. Egyptians believed in a world filled with gods and goddesses who managed different aspects of life. Some deities were connected to love and fertility, such as Hathor, often shown as a cow or a woman with cow horns. She represented love, joy, music, and motherhood. Another key figure was Isis, known for her devotion to her husband Osiris. Their myth is one of the best-known love stories in Ancient Egypt.

In the myth, Osiris is killed by his jealous brother Set. Grief-stricken Isis travels across Egypt, gathers Osiris's body parts, and restores him to life through magic. Although Osiris becomes the ruler of the Underworld, the love between Isis and Osiris symbolizes loyalty and devotion that conquers even death. This story influenced how Egyptians saw the strength of marital and familial bonds. The idea that love could extend beyond the grave was a central theme in Egyptian religion, contributing to funeral customs and beliefs about the afterlife.

Family Structure and Social Norms

Ancient Egyptian society placed a high value on family. Households often included parents, children, and sometimes extended relatives. Having children was generally seen as a blessing because they could care for aging parents and continue family traditions. Sons, especially, were expected to carry on the family line, but daughters also held important roles in many families. The stability of the home was considered a reflection of the order that Egyptians believed the gods desired.

Men and women each had defined roles, but there was also some flexibility compared to other ancient cultures. Women in Egypt could own property, inherit from their parents, and even initiate divorce in certain circumstances. This legal status gave women a degree of independence. Marriages were usually monogamous for commoners, although among royalty or high-status individuals, polygamy or secondary marriages sometimes occurred for political reasons or to ensure heirs.

Courtship and Choosing a Partner

While we do not have complete details of Egyptian courtship, some surviving love poems and personal letters give clues about how couples might have expressed romantic interest. In these texts, lovers speak of their affection with gentle words, describing each other's beauty and the joy of being together. One poem might praise a beloved's eyes, while another might compare a lover's voice to a sweet melody. These writings suggest that young people did experience romantic feelings and that love could be an important factor when seeking a spouse.

However, practical considerations also mattered. Families sometimes arranged marriages to secure property or strengthen ties with another household. Even in such cases, the couple's consent was often considered. Because women could hold property, a match benefited both sides if they united land and assets. There was no rigid "marriage ceremony" with official priests in the earliest periods; instead, a couple might simply agree to live together, sometimes recording the arrangement in a contract if property was involved.

Marriage Contracts and Property Rights

In the Middle and New Kingdom periods, written marriage contracts became more common, especially for people of higher status. These contracts laid out the rights of the husband and wife, such as who owned which piece of property, how inheritance would work, and what should happen in case of divorce. For example, a marriage contract might say that if the couple separated, the wife would keep her dowry, and any shared property would be divided in a certain way.

Though these details might seem practical, they show that love in Ancient Egypt was not separated from social and economic concerns. People wanted clear agreements to protect both parties, ensuring harmony and stability in a marriage. The existence of these contracts does not mean marriages lacked affection. Rather, it highlights the Egyptians' desire to bring order and clarity to every aspect of life, including personal relationships.

Royal Marriages and Political Alliances

Pharaohs and members of the royal family often married for political and dynastic reasons. In some cases, a king would marry his sister or half-sister to keep the royal bloodline pure, at least according to their beliefs. This practice might seem strange to us, but in Ancient Egypt, it was viewed as a way to maintain divine lineage and ensure loyalty within the family. Royal women, such as queens and princesses, could hold significant power. Queens like Nefertiti and Hatshepsut were influential in government and religious affairs.

Political alliances were also formed through marriage between Egyptian royalty and the children of foreign kings. Such unions helped secure peace treaties or alliances, turning love and marriage into tools of diplomacy. Whether or not true affection grew from these political marriages varied, but they reflect how love and duty could blend at the highest levels of power.

Love Poetry and Romantic Expression

Ancient Egypt produced a body of literature often referred to as "love poems" or "love songs." These were found on papyri and in tomb inscriptions. Though not always personal letters, these poems use first-person voices to express longing, admiration, and even playful teasing between lovers. They speak of secret meetings by the river, the thrill of a stolen kiss, and the sadness of being apart.

A typical poem might say something like, "My beloved's voice is sweet, more pleasing than fine oil." Another might declare, "I wish I could be the laundryman who washes my beloved's clothes, so I could be close to her every day." This style shows an intimate, emotional side of Egyptian culture. Though the poems are idealized, they suggest that Egyptians valued the deep personal feelings that connect two people in love.

Daily Life: Affection Between Spouses

Beyond poetry, everyday items such as letters, jewelry, and household goods reveal affection within marriage. Spouses would address each other with endearing terms in letters, expressing concern for health or excitement for a safe return from a trip. Some amulets were exchanged between partners, perhaps as tokens of affection or protection. Artwork in tombs and on household objects sometimes depicted couples sitting together, holding hands, or sharing a meal, reflecting harmony and tenderness.

Even in official statues, a wife might stand or sit close to her husband, with an arm around his shoulders. These artistic choices show closeness and unity within marriage. Of course, not every relationship was perfect; jealousy, disagreements, and divorce could occur. Still, the strong representation of loving couples in Egyptian art points to a cultural ideal that valued partnership and emotional ties.

Roles of Men and Women in Love

Although men typically headed the household, women in Ancient Egypt held notable legal and social power compared to many other ancient cultures. A wife could manage household finances, own businesses, and bring legal action if she felt wronged. This level of independence suggests that love might have been balanced by respect for each partner's role. The husband was expected to provide for and protect his family, while the wife kept the home running and raised the children. Together, they aimed to build a stable household that followed the principle of "ma'at," the Egyptian concept of cosmic order, truth, and balance.

While men had certain privileges, there is evidence that women did not hesitate to stand up for themselves. In cases of divorce, a wife could leave with her dowry, and if the husband was at fault, he might owe her additional compensation. This system, even if imperfect, likely reduced the power imbalance that we see in many other societies of the time. Love in this context had an element of mutual obligation and respect.

Children and the Family Bond

Children were highly valued in Ancient Egypt, both for practical reasons—such as caring for parents in old age—and emotional ones. Evidence from tomb paintings, personal letters, and educational materials suggests that parents took pride in nurturing and educating their children. Fathers often taught sons trades or farming techniques, while mothers showed daughters how to run a household. In wealthier families, a tutor or scribe might provide formal instruction.

Because Egyptians believed in a strong moral code, guided by religious principles, children were taught to honor their parents and maintain family dignity. Love for children can be seen in artwork that depicts parents playing with youngsters, feeding them, or holding them close. The emotional bond extended into the afterlife, where parents prayed that their children would continue the family line and keep their memory alive.

Jealousy, Divorce, and Relationship Challenges

Like all human societies, Ancient Egypt had its share of relationship problems. Jealousy, conflicts over property, or dissatisfaction with a spouse could lead to tension. Though social stability was highly valued, divorce was permitted. Sometimes a spouse might leave if the other committed adultery or neglected family duties. In certain records, we see references to court cases dealing with accusations of infidelity or property disputes. The existence of these cases shows that love and marriage were not always peaceful.

Divorce was relatively straightforward, especially if there was a marriage contract in place. The wife would typically take her dowry and any property that was rightfully hers. The husband might keep his own property. Children would often remain with the mother if they were very young, though arrangements varied. While divorce could be seen as a disruption of "ma'at," it was still a recognized solution to serious marital troubles.

Festivals and Public Celebrations of Love

The Egyptians loved festivals, which often included music, dancing, and feasting. Some of these events were dedicated to deities like Hathor or Isis, where themes of love, beauty, and fertility were front and center. People might gather at temples, offer gifts to the goddess, and pray for blessings in their personal relationships. Since many festivals were open to anyone, they brought communities together and possibly provided opportunities for young people to meet and form connections.

Music and dance were key parts of these celebrations. Temple dancers, called "musicians of the gods," performed routines that were both sacred and entertaining. The atmosphere of joy and communal bonding likely fostered a spirit of togetherness, reinforcing the idea that love was not just a private matter. It was linked to the divine plan and to the well-being of society as a whole.

The Afterlife and Eternal Love

One of the most distinctive features of Ancient Egyptian culture is the strong focus on the afterlife. Egyptians believed that death was a transition, not an end. They built elaborate tombs, stocked them with goods and food, and inscribed magical spells to help the deceased travel safely in the next world. Families stayed connected even after one member died, offering prayers and food at the tomb to sustain the departed spirit.

For married couples, the hope was that they would be reunited in the afterlife. Tomb art often depicted husband and wife together, continuing their love in eternity. Some tombs had dual burial chambers, or at least inscriptions that welcomed the surviving spouse to join the deceased in the future. Spells and texts sometimes included references to the couple's bond, ensuring that it would last beyond death. This desire to remain together forever is a poignant expression of love in Ancient Egypt, going beyond mere mortal life.

Love Myths and the Influence of Osiris and Isis

We have already mentioned the story of Osiris and Isis. Their devotion was a powerful symbol for how love could overcome misfortune. Another popular story involved Hathor, sometimes called the "Lady of Love," who protected couples and blessed them with joy. She was also believed to aid women in childbirth, linking romance, marriage, and family creation in a single divine figure.

By worshiping these deities, Egyptians connected their own relationships to cosmic powers, seeing love as part of the natural and divine order. Rituals, prayers, and offerings were not only about ensuring personal happiness but also about aligning with the universal balance that deities maintained. Love was seen as a force that kept families and society stable, just like the Nile's flood brought renewal each year.

Social Classes and Their Influence on Relationships

Egyptian society had distinct social classes, from the pharaoh at the top to nobles, scribes, artisans, farmers, and laborers, down to slaves or prisoners of war. People generally married within their social tier, although upward mobility was not impossible, especially for skilled artisans or scribes who might gain the favor of higher officials. In lower-class households, couples worked together in the fields or craft workshops, sharing responsibilities to support the family.

Among the wealthy, marriages could be arranged to preserve or increase family fortune. Still, evidence suggests that genuine affection could develop within these unions. Even in the tombs of high-ranking individuals, inscriptions often mention love and respect for a spouse. Some couples used phrases like "my beloved wife" or "my beloved husband" in official monuments, indicating that emotional attachment was present regardless of social status.

Personal Letters and Reflections on Love

Archaeologists have discovered personal letters written on papyrus or ostraca (pieces of broken pottery used for writing). Many of these messages relate to trade or government matters, but some include glimpses of personal life. A husband might write to his wife while traveling for work or military service, expressing longing and concern for her health. A wife might instruct her husband to bring certain items home or remind him to stay safe.

In these letters, we see the daily realities of love in Ancient Egypt: the worry over physical distance, the need for reassurance, and the practical tasks that each spouse handled. The tone is often caring. Phrases like "Do not forget me" or "May you be well in the sight of the gods" show tenderness and emotional connection, even though the language can be formal.

Sexuality and Physical Affection

Ancient Egyptians had a relatively open view of physical affection, especially within marriage. Art often showed couples embracing or touching affectionately. Some love poems are frank about desire, suggesting a culture that accepted physical intimacy as a natural and positive part of life. However, public behavior was probably still modest, especially in more formal settings.

Temple decorations sometimes included images that symbolized fertility, and certain festivals encouraged sexual vitality. This openness, however, coexisted with norms that required individuals to honor their family and community. Adultery was frowned upon and could lead to legal trouble, especially if it disrupted household harmony. Overall, sexuality was seen as a gift from the gods, with boundaries set by social values and religious beliefs.

Magic, Amulets, and Love Spells

Magic was woven into everyday Egyptian life. People used spells and charms for protection, health, and sometimes for love. There are texts called "love spells" or "incantations" that people might recite to gain someone's affection or to keep a partner faithful. These spells often appealed to deities like Hathor or used symbols connected to love and desire.

For instance, an amulet might be worn to draw the attention of a desired partner or to strengthen an existing union. Another might be placed under a spouse's bed to guard against infidelity. While we cannot say how common these practices were, the very existence of such spells and charms shows that Egyptians recognized the complexity of human emotions. They believed in using spiritual help to guide and protect their relationships.

Continuity and Change Over the Centuries

Ancient Egypt is not just one static period; it went through the Old Kingdom, Middle Kingdom, New Kingdom, and various intermediate periods over thousands of years. Over time, customs related to love and marriage evolved, especially when foreign powers like the Hyksos, Nubians, or later the Greeks and Romans held influence. Still, the core ideas of partnership, family stability, and a connection to divine order stayed strong.

Texts from the Ptolemaic period (after Alexander the Great's conquest) show a mixing of Greek and Egyptian traditions. Marriages could incorporate Greek customs, but many Egyptian beliefs about the afterlife and divine protection of the home remained. This continuity hints at the deep roots that love, marriage, and family had in the Egyptian mindset.

CHAPTER 4

LOVE IN BIBLICAL TIMES

Biblical times span a large historical period and include the cultural contexts of ancient Israel and nearby regions. For the purposes of this chapter, we will focus mainly on the Hebrew Bible (also known as the Old Testament) and how it shaped ideas about love, marriage, family, and covenant relationships. We will look at how the patriarchal family structure operated, how traditions and laws influenced romantic and familial love, and how scripture preserved personal expressions of devotion—most famously in texts like the Song of Songs.

The Patriarchal Background

In the narratives of the Hebrew Bible, family life often revolved around a patriarch—an elder male figure, such as Abraham, Isaac, or Jacob, who led the household. This extended household could include multiple generations living under one roof. It also included servants, herds, and property. Love in this context was not just about individual emotion; it was tied to family honor, lineage, and survival in a challenging environment.

God's covenant with the people of Israel frequently used family language, highlighting the importance of offspring and inheritance. Promises from God often took the form of "descendants as numerous as the stars." This stress on fertility meant that marriage and childbearing were central concerns for many families. A loving and fruitful marriage was seen as a blessing from God, connecting human relationships to divine plans.

Marriage as a Social and Covenant Bond

Marriages in biblical times involved negotiations between families. A bride price (also called mohar) was commonly paid by the groom's family to the bride's family, reflecting both the value placed on the bride and a form of financial security. Arranged marriages were normal, with fathers or older male relatives taking the lead in deciding suitable matches. The couple's feelings could still matter. For example, the biblical story of Jacob's love for Rachel shows a man deeply smitten, willing to work seven years (which turned into fourteen) to marry her. This indicates that strong romantic emotion was acknowledged, even if family negotiations were still in play.

In many biblical accounts, marriage is presented as a sacred bond, sometimes described with covenant language. The relationship between God and Israel is likened to that of a husband and wife, implying loyalty, devotion, and exclusive commitment. This view shaped how adultery was understood: unfaithfulness in marriage paralleled unfaithfulness to God. Therefore, preserving marital fidelity was both a social and spiritual duty.

Polygamy and Concubines

Some prominent biblical figures had multiple wives or concubines. Abraham had Sarah and later took Hagar as a concubine to produce an heir. Jacob had two wives—Leah and Rachel—and also fathered children with their maidservants. King David and King Solomon famously had multiple wives, with Solomon's marriages often for political alliances. The acceptance of polygamy in certain biblical narratives can feel at odds with later Judeo-Christian norms of monogamy. However, it reflects the historical context of ancient Near Eastern societies, where preserving family lines and forming alliances were vital.

These arrangements were not always peaceful. Stories show jealousy, rivalry between wives, and complicated family dynamics. The biblical text often highlights the emotional struggles that come from such relationships, as in the tensions between Sarah and Hagar, or between Leah and Rachel. Despite these complications, the biblical world accepted polygamy as part of family life for those who could afford it or had social reasons to keep multiple partners.

Love in the Song of Songs

Perhaps the most direct expression of romantic love in the Hebrew Bible is found in the Song of Songs (also known as the Song of Solomon). This short collection of poems is filled with imagery of lovers praising each other's beauty, longing for one another, and enjoying each other's company. The language is earthy and vivid, using nature metaphors—like describing the beloved's eyes as doves or comparing her lips to a scarlet thread. Unlike many other biblical texts that focus on laws or historical events, the Song of Songs is purely poetic, celebrating human desire and mutual affection.

Although the Song of Songs has been interpreted in various ways—some see it as an allegory for God's love for Israel or Christ's love for the Church—the plain sense of the text is a celebration of romantic love. This indicates that biblical culture was capable of embracing the more emotional and passionate aspects of human relationships. The presence of such poetry in scripture shows that love was not only about social contracts or procreation; it was also about personal delight, tenderness, and devotion.

Laws Related to Marriage and Family

Several biblical laws address marriage, divorce, and sexual conduct. For example, Deuteronomy 24:1-4 discusses the granting of a certificate of divorce if a husband finds something "indecent" about his wife. The details are sparse, but it indicates that divorce was possible under certain conditions. Other passages in the Torah talk about what happens if a man violates a woman, or if a widow is left childless. The practice of "levirate marriage" required a deceased man's brother to marry the widow to provide an heir for the deceased, ensuring the family line continued.

These laws emphasize the idea that marriage was deeply intertwined with the social order. Love mattered, but so did family honor, tribal identity, and property rights. The concern for preserving a family's name and land holdings was so strong that it shaped the entire legal approach to relationships. Yet even within these constraints, personal affection could blossom, as biblical stories of couples sometimes reveal.

Examples of Romantic Devotion

Beyond the Song of Songs, there are stories that hint at strong romantic feelings. Jacob's deep love for Rachel stands out. He served her father Laban for seven years to marry her, was tricked into marrying her sister Leah, then worked an additional seven years to secure Rachel's hand. His devotion is highlighted in the text, showing that biblical writers recognized passionate love as a powerful force. Another example might be the story of Elkanah and Hannah (1 Samuel 1), where Elkanah tries to comfort Hannah when she struggles with infertility, showing a caring attitude toward his wife's emotional pain.

Such narratives balance the broader perspective that marriage was part of a social and legal framework. They remind us that even in an era of arranged unions and strong patriarchal structures, people could still experience and express genuine affection, empathy, and devotion within marriage.

The Role of Women in Biblical Love

Women in biblical times often had fewer legal rights than men, though their influence within the family could be substantial. Wives and mothers were key to managing the household, bearing children, and preserving traditions. Some women in the Bible, such as Ruth, Esther, and Abigail, played pivotal roles that extended beyond the domestic sphere. Ruth's story, for instance, highlights her loyalty to her mother-in-law Naomi and leads her to marry Boaz. Ruth's actions demonstrate both steadfast love and resourcefulness, showing that women could shape their own destinies within the cultural limits.

In relationships, women's perspectives are sometimes voiced, though biblical texts are mostly written from a male viewpoint. Still, we see hints of women's feelings. Leah and Rachel compete for Jacob's attention, each longing for love and recognition. Hannah prays fervently for a child, expressing her distress openly. These moments show women as active participants in the emotional dimensions of love, not mere bystanders.

Courtship and Betrothal

Formal courtship as we imagine it today did not necessarily exist in the same way in biblical times. Betrothal involved an agreement that was legally binding even before the couple lived together. Families might negotiate the bride price, the timing of the wedding feast, and other details, often with input from the potential bride and groom. Once betrothed, the bride was considered effectively "married," even though the couple had not yet consummated the union or begun living together. Breaking a betrothal could be seen as adultery, reflecting the serious nature of these agreements.

Yet, biblical narratives do offer glimpses of affectionate gestures. For instance, in the story of Isaac and Rebekah (Genesis 24), Abraham's servant travels to find a wife for Isaac. Rebekah shows kindness by offering water to the servant and his camels, reflecting a gentle and generous spirit. Though it is a family-arranged match, the text implies that Isaac is comforted by Rebekah's presence, suggesting emotional warmth in the relationship.

Love for Children and Family Bonds

Like many ancient cultures, biblical society saw children as a blessing from God, essential to continuing the family line and fulfilling divine commands to "be fruitful and multiply." Parents were expected to love and instruct their children in religious practices and moral behavior. The famous passage in Deuteronomy 6:4-9, known as the Shema, instructs parents to teach God's laws to their children diligently. This teaching process was an expression of parental love, ensuring the next generation would uphold the covenant.

Stories like that of Joseph and his father Jacob (Israel) in Genesis highlight a father's deep love for a favored son, which unfortunately causes jealousy among the other brothers. The emotional highs and lows in these family dramas show how love could be a source of both unity and conflict. Despite the tensions, the biblical accounts often end with reconciliation and forgiveness, indicating that family love was ultimately meant to triumph over strife.

Friendship and Brotherly Love

Love in biblical times was not limited to marriage and family. Friendships also held deep significance. One of the most famous examples is the bond between David and Jonathan. The Bible describes their souls as being "knit" together (1 Samuel 18:1), and they formed a covenant that involved loyalty and self-sacrifice. Jonathan even risked his relationship with his father, King Saul, to protect David. Their friendship stands as a powerful example of mutual love and devotion outside of marriage ties.

In many parts of the Hebrew Bible, the command to "love your neighbor as yourself" (Leviticus 19:18) is emphasized, showing that love was seen as an ethical principle guiding social relationships. This did not always refer to romantic love but rather to compassion, fairness, and solidarity among community members. Even strangers and sojourners in the land were to be treated with kindness.

Adultery and Jealousy

Adultery was condemned in biblical law and was sometimes punishable by death (Leviticus 20:10, Deuteronomy 22:22). The severity of the punishment shows how seriously biblical society took marital faithfulness. Such laws aimed to protect family integrity and inheritance lines. Jealousy was also recognized as a potent force. There is even a specific ritual described in Numbers 5:11–31 dealing with a husband's suspicion of his wife's unfaithfulness, reflecting concern over maintaining marital purity.

While the text does not always reveal how spouses navigated ordinary jealousy, the existence of these strict rules indicates that controlling sexual behavior was a major concern. Love and marriage were thus bound by moral and communal guidelines, aiming to keep the entire community in right relationship with God.

Romance in a Harsh Environment

It is worth noting that biblical times included periods of nomadic life, settling in Canaan, enslavement in Egypt, wandering in the desert, and eventually the establishment of the kingdoms of Israel and Judah. Wars, famines, and political upheaval were common. In such challenging conditions, marriage and family bonds took on extra importance. A husband and wife depended on each other not only for emotional support but also for practical survival—tending flocks, managing farms, raising children, and defending property.

Love, in this sense, was both a comfort in difficult times and a crucial element for continuity. While romantic love might not have been the sole foundation of marriage in many cases, it played a role in strengthening the partnership. Stories like that of Boaz and Ruth, where Boaz acts protectively and kindly, demonstrate how compassion and caring could guide relationships in a harsh environment.

The Influence of Other Ancient Near Eastern Cultures

The Hebrew people did not live in isolation. They interacted with neighboring cultures like the Canaanites, Egyptians, Assyrians, and Babylonians. Some biblical laws and narratives may have parallels in older Mesopotamian texts, as we saw in Chapter 2. For instance, the Code of Hammurabi contains laws about marriage, inheritance, and family honor. While biblical law had distinct features, it existed within a broader legal and cultural setting of the ancient Near East.

The worship of other gods by neighboring peoples is also a theme in the Bible, often described as spiritual adultery when Israelites strayed from their own God. This language again ties romantic or marital fidelity to faithfulness in religion. The biblical authors viewed loyalty in love and loyalty to God as closely connected. This is a recurring metaphor that shaped how people saw both personal relationships and national identity.

Expressions of Affection in the Psalms and Proverbs

Though the Psalms are mostly hymns and prayers, some verses express love for God in highly personal terms, showing deep emotional devotion. While this is not romantic love, it reveals how the biblical mindset saw love as central to all relationships, including the divine-human bond. The Book of Proverbs, meanwhile, contains wisdom about relationships—urging husbands and wives to be faithful, children to respect parents, and friends to be loyal. These writings do not always describe romance in a detailed way, but they underline virtues like kindness, generosity, and respect, which foster loving relationships.

Divorce and Its Consequences

While Old Testament law permitted divorce, it was generally discouraged. Malachi 2:16 contains a phrase sometimes translated as "God hates divorce," suggesting that breaking a marriage covenant was a serious matter. Nonetheless, divorce was a legal procedure, more accessible to men than women, although a woman's family might intervene on her behalf if she was unfairly treated. This imbalance shows that patriarchal norms still heavily shaped marital dynamics, even if love and mutual respect were cultural ideals.

Over time, Jewish interpretations of these laws evolved, but during the biblical era, the main concern was keeping social order and honoring God's commands. Love was important, but it was woven into a strict social and religious framework that left less room for individual choice than we might see in later periods.

The Legacy of Biblical Love

The Hebrew Bible's teachings on love, marriage, and family would have a lasting impact on Western culture, shaping Jewish and, later, Christian and Islamic views on relationships. Phrases like "love your neighbor as yourself" remain central moral guidelines. The image of marriage as a covenant has influenced how many societies view the seriousness of wedding vows. Stories like Jacob and Rachel, Ruth and Boaz, and David and Jonathan continue to be read as examples of dedication and faithfulness.

While modern readers might question some of the patriarchal practices or the acceptance of polygamy, it is important to see these elements in their historical context. Love in biblical times had to function within a world of extended families, clan alliances, tribal conflicts, and a developing moral and legal system. Yet despite these constraints, biblical narratives and laws still acknowledge that love is a powerful and transformative force.

CHAPTER 5

LOVE IN ANCIENT GREECE

Ancient Greece was made up of many independent city-states, each with its own traditions and styles of government, but they shared a common language and cultural identity. These city-states included places like Athens, Sparta, Corinth, and Thebes. Though they competed politically and militarily, they were united by religion, festivals, myths, and beliefs about the gods. Love in Ancient Greece was influenced by many factors: social structures, philosophical ideas, stories of the gods, and the daily life of the citizens. In this chapter, we will explore how the Greeks thought about different types of love, how they formed families, how philosophers examined love, and how myths and art expressed the power of this feeling.

The Many Words for Love

The Greek language recognized that love took many forms. Modern scholars often point to four main words that capture different shades of love:

1. **Eros**: This was the form of love most closely associated with physical desire and attraction. Eros could be intense, passionate, and sometimes overwhelming. The Greeks saw it as a powerful force that could inspire bravery but also lead to impulsive actions.

2. **Philia**: This meant friendship or a strong bond based on loyalty and shared experiences. Philia existed between friends, family members, and those who fought side by side. It often implied mutual respect and caring.

3. **Agape**: This referred to a more selfless, universal kind of love. Although it became more prominent in later periods (especially in Christian writings), the Greeks had a concept of generous love or goodwill toward others.

4. **Storge**: This was natural affection, often used for the love between parents and children or the fondness people had for close kin.

These words show that the Greeks understood love as more than just romance. It included friendship, family devotion, passionate desire, and wider goodwill. While we might not see all these words equally in the surviving texts, they help us see that Greek culture had a nuanced view of love.

The Influence of the Gods

Greek religion was polytheistic, with gods who acted in ways that seemed both powerful and very human. Many myths show gods falling in love, experiencing jealousy, or engaging in power struggles. The gods had complicated relationships among themselves and sometimes with mortals. For example, Zeus, the king of the gods, was often involved in affairs with mortal women, leading to legendary heroes like Hercules or Perseus. Aphrodite was the goddess of love and beauty, often portrayed as a force that could stir desire in gods and humans alike.

These stories influenced how people thought about love. If the gods, who were immortal and mighty, could be driven by desire or heartbreak, then love was a universal power. Myths also taught lessons about consequences. When gods like Hera became jealous, tragedy could follow. This served as a reminder that love, while beautiful, could bring challenges. Poets, playwrights, and artists drew on these myths to explore the nature of love and to entertain and educate the Greek people.

Courtship and Marriage Customs

In most Greek city-states, marriages were arranged by families. A father or male guardian would choose a suitable husband for a girl. She might have had some input, but often, the match was based on social and financial considerations. Marriage was seen as a way to produce legitimate children who would inherit property and continue the family line. Love in the modern romantic sense was not always the main purpose of marriage, though affection could certainly grow between spouses.

The ideal age for marriage differed between men and women. Women usually married in their early to mid-teens, while men might marry later, often in their late twenties. This age gap reflected the idea that a man should first establish himself, gain some stability, and then start a family. Once a marriage was agreed upon, a betrothal took place, which was a formal contract. Gifts and dowries could be exchanged. The bride's family might provide a dowry of money, land, or personal items, ensuring the bride's security in her husband's household.

Wedding ceremonies involved rituals to honor the gods. Brides might bathe in sacred water, and both families prayed to deities like Hera (associated with marriage) or Artemis (associated with transitions for young women). A feast would follow, and after that, the bride was led in a ceremonial procession to her husband's home. This was a moment of celebration but also a sign that she was leaving her father's house to join a new family.

Despite these formal customs, evidence suggests that personal affection could grow. Spouses sometimes wrote affectionate letters, dedicated inscriptions to each other, or showed concern in daily tasks. Many Greek epitaphs (inscriptions on tombstones) mention the deep love husbands and wives felt for each other, indicating that while marriages were often arranged, genuine emotional bonds were common.

The Role of Women in Greek Marriages

Athenian society, which is often the most studied, had strict ideas about women's roles. Respectable women were expected to stay at home, manage the household, and bear children. They had limited freedom to move in public spaces, though they could attend some religious festivals. In other city-states, such as Sparta, women had more freedom, could own land, and took part in physical training. But across Greece, women were generally under the authority of a male relative.

Despite these limitations, women could influence family life. They managed household finances, supervised servants, and were responsible for educating children in their earliest years. Archaeological findings like household records and women's personal possessions show that women managed many daily tasks. If love is seen partly as care and loyalty within a family, then Greek wives played a key part in maintaining those bonds.

However, women's legal status remained restricted. Divorce was possible but generally favored men. If a woman wanted to leave her husband, it could be challenging without a male guardian's help. Yet there were cases where women inherited property if there were no male heirs. Laws varied between city-states, but the overall picture shows that marriage for women meant a combination of duties and hopes for emotional stability.

Homosexual Relationships and the Concept of Pederasty

Ancient Greece is also known for its acceptance of certain same-sex relationships, especially between men. In some city-states, there was a social practice often referred to as pederasty, where an older man (the "erastes") formed a bond with a younger male (the "eromenos"), usually in his teens. This relationship was often seen as an educational mentorship that might include physical and emotional closeness. The older partner was supposed to guide the younger in moral, social, and even military matters, while the younger partner was expected to show respect.

Though these relationships sometimes involved physical intimacy, they were also regulated by social norms. Excessive displays of lust or improper behavior could be criticized. Philosophers like Plato wrote about these relationships, sometimes describing them as a higher form of love that inspired wisdom and virtue. However, the practice varied greatly across regions, and the details remain debated by scholars. It is important to note that while some Greeks saw such relationships as ideal, others might have disapproved or at least imposed strict guidelines on behavior.

Same-sex love also appeared among women, though less is recorded. The poet Sappho, from the island of Lesbos, wrote poems celebrating love between women. Little is known about how common or accepted female same-sex relationships were, but Sappho's surviving verses remain some of the earliest examples of women expressing romantic love for other women.

Philosophical Views on Love

Greek philosophers explored love in depth. They were not just interested in the feeling but also in its moral, ethical, and social implications. A few key figures include:

1. **Plato**: In works like the *Symposium* and the *Phaedrus*, Plato examines love (especially Eros) as a force that can lead the soul toward higher forms of beauty and truth. In the *Symposium*, different speakers share their views on love, culminating in Socrates' speech that describes Eros as a desire for the eternal form of beauty. Plato's idea of "Platonic love" emphasizes a bond that rises above mere physical desire to reach intellectual or spiritual connection. Although the dialogue centers on male-male

relationships common in Athenian society, it has been interpreted more broadly to describe love's potential to inspire virtue in any relationship.
2. **Aristotle**: In his works on ethics, Aristotle discusses "friendship" (philia) extensively. He sees friendship as essential for a good and happy life. While he talks less about romantic love, his ideas about mutual respect, shared values, and goodwill can apply to many forms of love. Aristotle identifies three types of friendship: those based on usefulness, those based on pleasure, and those based on virtue. A friendship based on virtue, he says, is the highest form, where each person wishes the good of the other for the other's sake.
3. **Epicurus**: In the Hellenistic period, Epicurus taught that pleasure and freedom from pain are the highest goods. He believed that stable friendships bring lasting happiness, but he warned against the intense passions of romantic love, seeing them as potential sources of pain or anxiety. For Epicurus, love was best enjoyed as a gentle companionship free from turmoil.
4. **The Stoics**: Stoic philosophers, like Zeno of Citium or later Epictetus, valued self-control and reason. They did not reject love, but they advised against becoming enslaved by passions. They felt that true love should be guided by virtue, not driven by uncontrolled emotion.

These philosophical discussions show that the Greeks were deeply concerned with questions about love, the soul, desire, and the pursuit of the good life. While some everyday people might not have studied these texts, the ideas often seeped into broader culture through conversations, education, and the works of playwrights.

Mythology and Love Stories

Greek myths are full of love stories that combine the mortal and divine. One famous example is the story of Eros (Cupid) and Psyche, though it appears more fully in Roman times under Apuleius. Still, the Greeks had earlier tales about the god Eros, who could shoot arrows that made gods and mortals fall in love instantly. Another story is that of Orpheus and Eurydice. Orpheus, a gifted musician, travels to the Underworld to bring back his beloved Eurydice, only to lose her at the last moment when he looks back too soon. This myth underscores the depth of devotion and the sorrow love can bring.

The Trojan War itself, central to Homer's *Iliad*, began because Paris of Troy fell in love with Helen, the wife of the Spartan king Menelaus. Helen's abduction or elopement triggered a massive conflict. This story reveals how powerful and disruptive love could be. Homer's epics also touch on the love between comrades, like Achilles and Patroclus, which plays a major role in Achilles' grief-driven rage.

Greek tragedy, too, often explored the darker side of love—jealousy, revenge, betrayal. In plays by Euripides or Sophocles, characters like Medea or Phaedra become tragic figures, showing how uncontrolled passion can lead to ruin. These stories entertained Greek audiences during festivals but also served as moral lessons about the potential dangers of intense desire or misplaced affection.

Love and Civic Life

In many Greek city-states, especially Athens, love was not only a private matter but also had connections to civic duty. Producing legitimate children was a responsibility because the state depended on new generations of citizens. In Athens, citizenship could pass only through male children born of legitimate marriages. Therefore, the way love and marriage were managed had a direct impact on the future of the city-state.

Festivals honored gods associated with fertility, such as Demeter and Dionysus. During these festivals, communities came together to celebrate with feasts, processions, and plays. Though these events were religious in nature, they also reinforced social bonds and sometimes opened spaces for personal encounters. Young men and women might meet each other, forging friendships or alliances that could lead to marriage.

Some city-states had public rituals or even songs dedicated to the virtues of love, friendship, and comradeship, especially in the military context. For instance, Sparta encouraged strong bonds among warriors, believing these ties could increase courage on the battlefield. Plato's *Symposium* even praises an army composed of lovers and their beloveds, suggesting that no one would act cowardly in front of someone they dearly love.

Sappho and the Lyric Poets

Sappho, who lived on the island of Lesbos in the 7th century BCE, is one of the earliest known female poets. Her poems celebrate passion and longing, often directed toward other women. Though much of her work survives only in fragments, her verses show deep emotional insight and a strong focus on personal experience. She uses vivid imagery to describe the power of love, comparing its effects on the body to physical trembling, burning, or loss of voice.

Other lyric poets of Ancient Greece, like Alcaeus (also from Lesbos), Anacreon, and Pindar, wrote about love, wine, and the joys of life. They performed their poems to the accompaniment of a lyre, making the experience both musical and poetic. These poems were shared during symposia—drinking parties where men reclined on couches, discussed politics, philosophy, and recited poetry. Such gatherings were key social events, and love was often a topic of conversation and performance.

Comedy and Love

Greek comedy, particularly in the works of Aristophanes, poked fun at romantic entanglements and social norms. Aristophanes often used satire and exaggerated scenarios to highlight the foolishness that can arise from love or lust. While these plays aimed to make people laugh, they also taught the audience to reflect on the absurdity of excessive desire, the challenges in marriage, and the potential conflicts between men and women. Comedy could be lighthearted or ribald, but it still offered social commentary on how love affected daily life.

In *Lysistrata*, for example, Aristophanes imagines women going on a sex strike to force their men to end a war. Though the play is not a romantic comedy in the modern sense, it showcases the power women can hold over men through withholding intimacy. It's a humorous scenario, but it also touches on real social dynamics of love, desire, and marital relationships in Ancient Greece.

The Daily Reality of Love

While myths and philosophers capture the grand ideas, the everyday experiences of ordinary Greeks also shaped their view of love. Most people lived in rural areas or small towns, working farms or small trades. They interacted with neighbors, formed friendships, and raised families. Love in such environments involved companionship, shared labor, raising children, and passing on traditions. Though ancient sources mostly come from elite or literary perspectives, we can still see glimpses of simple affection in things like small votive offerings to local gods, inscriptions on gravestones, and personal letters recovered by archaeologists.

When a loved one died, families performed elaborate funeral rites. Women often took the lead in mourning rituals, washing and anointing the body, and singing laments. These practices show that love extended into the realm of death, with the living expressing their devotion through memorials and ongoing visits to the graves of relatives. The bond between spouses or between parents and children did not vanish at death; it continued in memory and ritual.

Challenges and Conflicts

Like any society, Ancient Greece faced challenges that affected love and family life. Wars between city-states, such as the Peloponnesian War between Athens and Sparta, tore families apart. Men were away fighting for extended periods, leading to separation from their wives and children. Some never returned, creating widows who might have to remarry or rely on male relatives for support.

Economic hardships also impacted relationships. Dowries could become burdensome, and families might struggle to find good matches for their daughters. Sometimes marriages were used to form alliances, merging properties or forging political ties. In such circumstances, romance might have been secondary to survival or social strategy.

Greek drama and historical writings sometimes mention domestic quarrels or disputes over inheritance. These conflicts show that while love was idealized in poetry, real relationships could be complicated by jealousy, ambition, or simple disagreements. Yet, the strong emphasis on loyalty and mutual care, whether in friendships or marriages, suggests that the Greeks valued genuine affection as much as they valued strategy and rational thought.

Education and the Nurturing of Values

Education in Ancient Greece aimed to shape character as well as intellect. Boys, especially in Athens, studied literature, music, and physical training. They learned Homer's epics, which included themes of friendship, loyalty, and love. Through reciting these stories, they absorbed lessons about how heroes treated each other and the importance of standing by one's friends and family.

In Sparta, the education system (the "agoge") focused on developing strong warriors who also formed tight bonds with their comrades. Loyalty to the group was taught from a young age, reinforcing a sense of unity that some Spartans described as a form of deep friendship or love for one's peers. These educational frameworks reinforced cultural values about caring for those close to you, whether as family or as fellow citizens.

For girls, formal education was less common in most Greek cities, although some, like Sparta, did have structured training for women. Still, girls learned household tasks, childcare, and often how to read and recite certain texts. These skills allowed them to run a household effectively and pass on cultural values. Love within the family was nurtured through everyday living, shared religious festivals, and the moral lessons taught by mothers and other female relatives.

The Transition to the Hellenistic Period

By the fourth century BCE, Greece went through major political changes. After decades of internal conflict, the rise of Macedon under King Philip II and later his son, Alexander the Great, shifted the center of power. Alexander's conquests spread Greek culture far beyond the traditional boundaries, reaching Egypt, Persia, and parts of India. In this time, often called the Hellenistic period, Greek ideas about love, marriage, and relationships began to mix with the customs of other cultures.

New kingdoms were established, and the role of Greek language and philosophy expanded. Scholars, poets, and philosophers gathered in new cultural centers like Alexandria in Egypt. Under these conditions, love continued to evolve as a subject of literary and philosophical interest. People from different backgrounds interacted, sometimes marrying across cultural lines, leading to unique blends of tradition. This mixing had a big effect on how love was expressed, both in personal life and in literature.

However, the core Greek values about relationships, the different words for love, and the influence of myth and philosophy remained strong. They adapted to new environments without losing their essence. By the time of the Hellenistic age, Greek thought about love included older traditions plus fresh viewpoints shaped by contact with distant lands.

CHAPTER 6

LOVE IN THE HELLENISTIC WORLD

The Hellenistic period began after the conquests of Alexander the Great in the late fourth century BCE. Following his death in 323 BCE, Alexander's vast empire was divided among his generals, giving rise to several Hellenistic kingdoms, such as the Ptolemaic Kingdom in Egypt, the Seleucid Empire in the Near East, and the Antigonid dynasty in Macedonia. During this era, Greek culture and language spread far beyond the traditional Greek city-states, mingling with local traditions from North Africa to Southwest Asia.

Love in the Hellenistic world took on new dimensions as people from different backgrounds interacted. Philosophical schools developed new ideas, poets found fresh inspirations, and the social fabric of these new kingdoms offered diverse ways to form relationships. In this chapter, we will look at how these cultural blends shaped love, family life, and personal bonds, and how new philosophies approached human affection.

The Legacy of Alexander the Great

Alexander's campaigns had two main effects on the concept of love:

1. **Cultural Blending**: Alexander's troops settled in conquered regions, taking local spouses and mixing Greek customs with Persian, Egyptian, and other traditions. This resulted in families that identified with both Greek culture and local ways, influencing marriage rituals, dowry practices, and ideas about romantic bonds.
2. **Political Marriages**: Alexander himself married women from different regions—Roxana from Bactria, and later Stateira (the daughter of the Persian king Darius III). By marrying into local royal families, he aimed to unify diverse peoples under his rule. These marriages were partly political, but they also brought new views on cross-cultural relationships into the spotlight. After Alexander's death, his successors often continued the practice, using marriage to form or solidify alliances.

The concept of love in these unions was complicated. While some of these marriages were arranged for political reasons, personal affection might have grown. Local customs about weddings and familial duties mixed with Greek expectations, producing hybrid traditions.

Hellenistic Kingdoms and Their Social Structures

The major Hellenistic kingdoms included:

- The **Ptolemaic Kingdom** in Egypt, ruled by the Ptolemy dynasty. They adopted many Egyptian customs but kept Greek as the language of administration.
- The **Seleucid Empire**, which spanned a vast territory from Asia Minor to parts of India. This region contained many different peoples and traditions, making it a melting pot of cultures.
- The **Antigonid** dynasty in Macedonia, which maintained a more traditional Greek identity but still interacted with neighboring regions.

In these kingdoms, Greek settlers lived alongside local populations. They built new cities, like Alexandria in Egypt and Seleucia on the Tigris, often designed with Greek-style architecture. However, local gods, traditions, and laws did not disappear. Instead, many cultural practices existed side by side or gradually mixed. As a result, love, marriage, and family life varied widely, depending on one's background and location.

Still, the Greek language (Koine Greek) became a common tongue for trade, administration, and literature. Philosophical schools spread into these new cities, bringing Greek theories on ethics and love. People might pray to both Greek gods, like Aphrodite, and local deities associated with love or fertility. This blend shaped how couples approached relationships, how they celebrated weddings, and how they honored the birth of children.

Philosophical Schools and Evolving Ideas of Love

During the Hellenistic period, older philosophical traditions continued, but new schools emerged or gained prominence. Each had its own view of love, emotion, and the meaning of life:

1. **Stoicism**: Founded by Zeno of Citium, Stoicism taught that virtue is the highest good, and emotions should be guided by reason. Stoics did not reject love outright, but they were wary of excessive passion, believing it could disturb one's inner peace. They supported a form of love that was rational, recognizing the moral worth of the beloved. If two individuals shared virtue, their bond could be strong. However, they advised not becoming so attached that one could not bear loss or heartbreak.
2. **Epicureanism**: Epicurus focused on seeking pleasure and avoiding pain. While Epicureans valued friendship highly, they saw romantic passions as risky because they could lead to jealousy, heartbreak, or other forms of emotional distress. They believed a quiet life of moderate pleasure and strong friendships was preferable to the intense emotional swings often brought by passionate love.
3. **Cynicism**: Cynics, following the example of Diogenes of Sinope, rejected many social conventions. They believed in living according to nature, which sometimes meant scorning marriage, wealth, and other societal norms. While they did not produce a detailed theory of love, their emphasis on independence suggested that emotional attachments could be a distraction from a simple, virtuous life.
4. **Platonists and Aristotelians**: Scholars who followed Plato or Aristotle continued to debate the nature of love. They worked in places like the Library of Alexandria, writing commentaries on older texts. Platonic ideas about rising from physical desire to a higher appreciation of beauty and virtue remained influential. Aristotelians still emphasized the importance of friendship and virtue in achieving happiness.

These schools did not exist in isolation. People living in cosmopolitan cities like Alexandria could encounter different philosophical ideas, sometimes blending them in personal ways. Love became part of a larger debate about how to live the best life possible.

The Role of Alexandria and Other Cultural Centers

Alexandria in Egypt was founded by Alexander the Great and became a major center of learning and culture. It hosted the famous Library of Alexandria and attracted scholars, poets, and thinkers from across the Mediterranean and beyond. This environment led to a creative explosion. New forms of poetry, called **Alexandrian poetry**, emerged, often exploring personal feelings and everyday experiences, including love.

Poets like **Callimachus** and **Theocritus** wrote about love in a more intimate manner compared to the grand epics of earlier times. Theocritus's "idylls" often featured pastoral settings, shepherds singing about unrequited love or the joys of romance. These poems captured small moments of longing, affection, or heartbreak, showing that love could be gentle and personal rather than always dramatic or heroic.

Alexandria also had a diverse population: Greeks, Egyptians, Jews, and people from many other backgrounds. Interfaith and intercultural marriages likely took place, although records are spotty. Women in the Ptolemaic dynasty, like Cleopatra VII, used marriage and personal alliances for political power, but Cleopatra was also romantically involved with Julius Caesar and Mark Antony, reflecting how personal relationships could influence global politics at the time. While Cleopatra's story is often told from a Roman perspective, it reminds us that love and politics were tightly connected in the Hellenistic courts.

Changing Views of Marriage and Family

As Greek settlers spread across the Hellenistic kingdoms, they brought their traditions of dowries, arranged marriages, and legal contracts. Yet local customs also persisted. In Egypt, for instance, marriage contracts from this period sometimes combined Greek legal language with Egyptian formulas. Couples might promise loyalty to each other under the gaze of both Greek and Egyptian gods. Some documents give specific details about property division, showing that both partners had rights and responsibilities, though men generally held the main legal power.

In many cases, women of Greek heritage had somewhat better legal standing than in classical Athens, partly because the Hellenistic world was more diverse and flexible. While women were still expected to marry and bear children, some managed estates or ran businesses, especially if they came from wealthy families. Royal women, like the Ptolemaic queens, could hold significant influence. These shifting roles might have opened new possibilities for affection, partnership, and even romance, though the extent varied by social class.

Royal families set trends in some respects. The ruling dynasties in Egypt or Syria sometimes married siblings to keep power within the family, echoing older Egyptian royal customs. For most Greeks, this practice was shocking, but within the royal court, it was a way to protect dynastic claims. Love in these settings might exist, but political motives usually overshadowed personal desires.

Cross-Cultural Romance

With trade routes expanding across the Mediterranean and into Asia, people traveled widely, sometimes settling far from their homelands. Merchants, soldiers, and government officials might marry local women, forming families that blended Greek language and customs with the traditions of the host culture. For example, a Greek soldier stationed in Bactria (part of modern Afghanistan) might take a local wife, raising children who learned both Greek and local languages.

These mixed families left behind inscriptions, coins, and other artifacts showing how love crossed cultural boundaries. Some would adopt Greek names or worship Greek gods alongside local deities. The children of such unions might identify with multiple traditions, creating a rich cultural tapestry. Love was thus not just a personal bond but also a bridge between peoples. While tensions could arise—some communities resisted Greek influence—numerous examples show that marriages between Greeks and non-Greeks did occur and sometimes thrived.

New Religious Movements and Mystery Cults

The Hellenistic period witnessed the rise or spread of various mystery cults and religious movements. These cults, dedicated to deities like Isis, Serapis, Cybele, Dionysus, or Mithras, offered personal religious experiences and sometimes promised a hopeful afterlife. Worship often involved secret rites that created a deep emotional connection among participants. Some cults emphasized the idea of divine love or union with a deity, suggesting that human love had a spiritual or cosmic aspect.

For example, the cult of Isis in Egypt portrayed the goddess as a loving wife and mother figure. She was revered for her devotion to Osiris, reflecting a myth of eternal love that overcame death. This myth, already important in Egyptian tradition, gained popularity among Greeks and other outsiders who settled in

Egypt. Worshipers saw Isis as a protective, nurturing figure whose love extended to humanity. In the mysteries, devotees felt a personal closeness to the goddess, blurring the line between divine and human love.

Likewise, the worship of Dionysus, which had existed in earlier Greek tradition, spread and changed form during the Hellenistic era. Dionysian rites involved ecstatic dancing, wine, and a sense of release from ordinary life. These gatherings could encourage strong bonds among participants, and, in some cases, they were associated with ideals of fellowship and shared emotional intensity. While not always described as "love" in the romantic sense, these collective experiences created unity and sometimes deep affection among worshipers.

Hellenistic Art and Expressions of Love

Art in the Hellenistic period took a new turn toward realism and emotional depth. Sculptures and paintings often showed ordinary people, not just gods or idealized athletes. This included scenes of family life, lovers embracing, or mothers with children. Some statues portrayed couples in tender poses, capturing human affection with more detail than in earlier classical art.

One example is the "Statue of Eros Sleeping," which highlights the innocence and vulnerability of the love-god. Instead of a powerful figure stirring passions, Eros appears as a tired child at rest, hinting at a gentler perspective on love's power. Other works depict everyday gestures of care, such as a woman looking into a small box of jewelry while a companion stands by, or couples walking together. These visual depictions suggest that artists and patrons valued intimate moments, seeing love as part of daily human experience.

In addition to sculpture, painted vases and mosaics might show courting scenes, banquets, or mythological lovers. The range of topics expanded, reflecting a society curious about personal emotions, private life, and the experiences of different social groups. From palaces to modest homes, art became a medium to explore the subtleties of love, desire, and companionship.

Literature and the Rise of the Novel

Another significant development in Hellenistic literary culture was the early form of the Greek novel or romance. While these works became more popular in the Roman period, some seeds were planted in the Hellenistic age. They told tales of young lovers separated by fate, traveling to distant lands, facing pirates, or other dangers, and ultimately reuniting. Such stories often emphasized the emotional bond between the protagonists, their steadfast loyalty, and the triumph of love against all odds.

Although many of these early prose romances are lost or only survive in fragments, the basic structure influenced later works. They combined adventure, emotional depth, and sometimes religious or philosophical messages. Love was the driving force, motivating characters to endure hardships and remain hopeful in the face of adversity. This narrative style—of star-crossed lovers on a journey—would become a staple of literature in the ancient world and beyond.

Women Writers and Poets in the Hellenistic Period

While men dominated most literary production, there were some women poets and writers in the Hellenistic age. One example is **Anyte of Tegea**, who wrote epigrams that touched on love and nature. She is often grouped with other poets of the Greek Anthology, which includes brief, insightful poems on various topics. Although not all of them are strictly about romantic love, some capture tender feelings or reflect on personal connections.

Another female poet was **Moero** of Byzantium, credited with writing epic and lyric poetry. Very little of her work survives, but references by ancient scholars suggest she tackled themes of myth and personal reflection. While we cannot be sure how much these women poets influenced broader ideas about love, their presence indicates that female voices existed in the cultural mix of the Hellenistic world. They added new perspectives to the discussion of affection, desire, and emotional expression.

Friendship and Civic Identity

Friendship remained an important form of love during the Hellenistic period, especially among Greek elites. The concept of *philia* extended beyond personal fondness to include political alliances and bonds within scholarly communities. Many intellectuals formed circles around great libraries or patron courts, forging friendships grounded in shared learning. These relationships often involved letter writing, gift exchanges, and mutual support.

Cities also used ideas of friendship on a civic scale. For instance, a city might form a "friendship" treaty with another city or a local ruler, using the language of bonds and loyalty. Although this was more diplomatic than personal, it reflects the Greek habit of describing strong ties as a kind of philia. The idea that love (or a form of it) could unify people was present not only in personal life but in the political and cultural fabric.

Challenges of the Hellenistic World

Life in the Hellenistic kingdoms was not always stable. Wars between successor states, taxation burdens, and local revolts caused upheaval. People sometimes migrated to avoid conflict or seek better opportunities. In uncertain times, love—whether familial, romantic, or platonic—became a source of comfort. Letters from that era occasionally mention worries about war, separation from loved ones, or the hope that spouses and children remained safe.

Merchants traveling long distances might be away from home for extended periods, similar to sailors or soldiers. Couples maintained ties through letters, many of which are lost, but a few have survived on papyrus. These personal documents sometimes mention longing for the beloved's embrace, the joy of receiving a child's drawing, or the relief of hearing news that everyone is well. Even in a big, ever-changing empire, the simple desire to love and be loved endured.

The Spread of Hellenistic Influence

As Greek culture blended with local ways, some societies adapted Greek forms of marriage or adopted Greek names for children. In places like Judea, where Jewish traditions were strong, Hellenistic influences led to internal debates about maintaining ancestral customs versus embracing "Greek ways." The Maccabean revolt in the 2nd century BCE was partly a reaction against forced Hellenization. Still, even in such regions, some individuals formed cross-cultural marriages. The love that developed in these situations might face criticism or social pressure, but it also proved that personal attachments could cross ethnic and religious lines.

In other areas, the influence was more peaceful. Local elites might send children to Greek-style schools, believing it would help them gain favor in the new kingdoms. These youths learned Greek language and possibly Greek myths about love and heroism. Over time, they passed on these ideas, creating a new generation that felt at home in both Greek and local traditions.

Legacy into the Roman Era

The Hellenistic period gradually gave way to Roman dominance. By the mid-1st century BCE, the Roman Republic began absorbing Hellenistic territories, culminating in the Roman Empire. Yet Greek culture did not vanish. Romans admired Greek art, philosophy, and literature, adopting many Hellenistic customs. Roman elites often spoke Greek as a second language, and Greek tutors taught their children. The Greek approach to love—articulate, philosophical, sometimes passionate—continued to influence Roman writers like Virgil, Ovid, and Plutarch.

In the eastern provinces of the Roman Empire, Greek remained a dominant language for centuries. Local people, now under Roman rule, carried forward the Hellenistic heritage. Philosophical schools in places like Athens and Rhodes persisted, shaping Roman thought on love, friendship, and virtue. The roots planted in the Hellenistic era thus continued to blossom, eventually feeding into late antique philosophies and even early Christian ideas about love and community.

CHAPTER 7

LOVE IN ANCIENT ROME

Ancient Rome began as a small city-state on the Italian peninsula and grew into a massive empire that stretched from Britain to North Africa and from Spain to the Near East. Over many centuries, Romans developed complex laws, institutions, and cultural values that affected every part of daily life—including love and marriage. Roman ideas about love were shaped by practical concerns (like property and social status) as well as by literature, philosophy, and religion. In this chapter, we will explore how the Romans thought about relationships, how marriage worked in different social classes, the role of legal frameworks, and how poets like Ovid added a new layer of romantic thought to the Roman world.

The Roman Family Structure

At the center of Roman society was the family, or *familia*. The head of the family, usually the eldest male, was called the *paterfamilias*. He had legal power over all family members, including his wife, children, and sometimes extended relatives. This authority was known as *patria potestas*, meaning "father's power." It gave the paterfamilias control over property, marriages, and even the life and death of family members in earlier times (though later laws limited these extremes).

Family structure influenced how love and marriage were arranged. While affection could certainly develop between spouses, Roman law and custom gave parents a major role in deciding who their children married. Since property and inheritance mattered so much, families often arranged marriages to protect or grow wealth, forge alliances, or increase social prestige. Yet even in this formal system, we find evidence of emotional bonds, mutual care, and the desire for companionship within Roman households.

Marriage Customs and Types of Marriages

Romans practiced different types of marriage, each with its own legal implications:

1. **Cum manu Marriage**: In early Rome, a wife who married *cum manu* came under the legal authority of her husband (or, in some cases, her husband's father). She legally became part of her husband's family, leaving behind her birth family. Any property she had might transfer to her husband's control. Over time, this form of marriage became less common.
2. **Sine manu Marriage**: In later periods, a wife usually remained under her father's authority rather than her husband's. This was called *sine manu* marriage. A woman in a *sine manu* marriage kept control of any property she inherited, and when her father died, she became legally independent if there was no other guardian. This arrangement gave women more autonomy, at least in theory, and often benefited their birth families by keeping property under the father's lineage.
3. **Contubernium**: This was an informal union commonly found among slaves or between a free person and a slave. Since slaves had no legal rights, they could not contract a proper marriage. But they might live as a couple in a relationship recognized by the community, if not by formal law.

To formalize a marriage, Romans often held a ceremony with witnesses. In a traditional wedding, the bride might wear a special dress and a flame-colored veil (*flammeum*). She was then led to her husband's house, sometimes through a procession that symbolized her transition from her father's home to her new household. Feasting and rituals would follow, including prayers to the gods for fertility and a prosperous family life.

Although these customs sound ceremonial, legal and social outcomes were paramount. Love, in the romantic sense, was not always the main motivator. Still, Roman letters, epitaphs, and personal writings show that married couples could share deep affection and loyalty.

Women's Roles and Responsibilities

Roman wives were in charge of running the household if they were freeborn and married into a respectable family. They oversaw servants, managed day-to-day finances, and cared for children's early upbringing. While Roman women lacked many political rights, some from wealthy or influential families could wield indirect power through family alliances or by advising their husbands. In the late Republic and early Empire, a few high-status women became quite influential, participating in social and sometimes political life, though never in official positions.

Because of *sine manu* marriage, some Roman women maintained their own property. They could inherit from their fathers and keep control of their dowries, which made them more independent than women in certain other ancient societies. A woman might sponsor building projects, religious events, or philanthropic works if she had enough resources. Still, her primary social role was tied to family and household duties, and she was expected to uphold her family's honor through modest behavior.

In this context, love between spouses sometimes blossomed as a partnership, with the wife acting as a capable household manager and the husband respecting her judgment. Literary sources mention husbands praising their wives' virtues, loyalty, and good management. Of course, not all marriages were harmonious; there were divorces, infidelities, and personal tragedies as well. But the ideal Roman marriage, at least in upper-class circles, was one of cooperation and mutual respect—where love could have a firm place, even if overshadowed by legal and social frameworks.

Divorce and Remarriage

Divorce was relatively easy for Romans. Since marriage was often understood as a matter of mutual consent, it could end when that consent ended. A man or a woman could initiate a divorce, though in practice men had more social freedom to do so. One common formula was for the person ending the marriage to say, "*Keep what is yours to yourself.*" No legal proceedings were always necessary, especially under *sine manu* arrangements, though returning the dowry or handling property could become complicated.

Remarriage was frequent, particularly in upper-class families. Women might marry multiple times in their lifetimes, especially if their husbands died or if families saw a strategic advantage in forming a new match. Men, too, often remarried, sometimes to secure an heir or to reinforce an alliance. This fluid approach to marriage does not mean Romans lacked commitment; rather, it reflects a society where practical concerns and family strategy were deeply entwined with personal life.

Love in Roman Literature

While Roman society was practical about marriage, poets and writers explored love more freely. One of the most famous voices on love was **Ovid**, whose works like the *Amores* and the *Ars Amatoria* (The Art of Love) offered witty, playful insights on romantic and erotic relationships. Ovid wrote about seduction, jealousy, and the thrill of secret affairs. His poetry sometimes clashed with the moral reforms of Emperor Augustus, who wanted to promote traditional family values. Ovid's eventual exile is often linked—at least in part—to the emperor's disapproval of his scandalous views on love (though the exact reasons remain debated).

Other poets, like **Catullus**, expressed intense emotional highs and lows in love. Catullus's poetry about "Lesbia" (a pseudonym for his real-life love interest) reveals passionate devotion, heartbreak, anger, and longing. These works show that Roman lovers, at least in the literary world, could be driven by powerful feelings similar to what we might recognize as romantic love today.

In addition to poetry, Roman plays (influenced by Greek drama) often focused on love plots, including comedic misunderstandings and mistaken identities. These stories sometimes featured young lovers opposing parental authority, reflecting tensions between romantic desire and arranged marriages. Audiences enjoyed watching the trials and tribulations of couples on stage, revealing a cultural appetite for love stories, even if real life was more pragmatic.

Philosophical Views on Love

Romans inherited Greek philosophical traditions, so Stoicism, Epicureanism, and other schools remained influential. Roman Stoics, such as Seneca and Marcus Aurelius, wrote about the importance of self-control and virtue. They believed love should be guided by reason and not by reckless passion. Stoicism did not prohibit love, but it warned against becoming enslaved by emotions. Compassionate and considerate relationships were fine, as long as they rested on virtue and rational conduct.

Epicureans in Rome, like their Greek counterparts, suggested that while friendships bring pleasure, romantic entanglements can cause distress and emotional turmoil. A moderate approach to all desires, they believed, would lead to a more stable life. Still, many Romans—both Stoics and Epicureans—took spouses and formed normal family relationships. Philosophy offered guidelines but did not prevent them from experiencing love and emotional ties.

There were also **Cynics** in Rome, although less prominent. Cynics often rejected social conventions and might question the idea of marriage altogether. They saw it as a distraction from a simpler, more "natural" life. Yet the mainstream of Roman society was more comfortable with structured families, which were key to passing on property and social status.

Adultery and Social Norms

Adultery was taken seriously in Rome, particularly when it involved a married woman. If a wife was caught in an affair, her husband could divorce her, and she could lose her dowry or face legal penalties. By contrast, a man's extramarital liaisons with slaves or lower-status individuals were often overlooked, reflecting a double standard. This does not mean men had absolute freedom; an affair with another man's wife or with a high-status woman could still cause scandal or result in legal trouble. But the moral emphasis and legal consequences usually fell harder on women.

During the reign of Emperor Augustus, new laws sought to regulate morality and increase the birthrate among the upper classes. These laws penalized adultery, rewarded marriage, and offered benefits to couples who produced children. Augustus believed that the moral and social health of Rome depended on stable families. While these reforms affected behavior to some extent, they did not completely end extramarital affairs. Roman literature and letters still mention secret romances, betrayals, and jealous quarrels, indicating that passionate love and forbidden relationships continued beneath the surface of official rules.

Love Beyond Class Boundaries

Roman society was divided into classes: **patricians** (aristocratic families), **plebeians** (common folk), **freedpersons** (former slaves who were freed), and slaves. Marriages typically happened within one's social class, especially for patricians who wanted to preserve noble bloodlines. However, in the wider population, there was more flexibility. Freedmen and freedwomen could marry each other or sometimes marry freeborn individuals, though social stigma might remain. Slaves, as mentioned, could not legally marry but formed informal unions (*contubernium*).

Some high-profile individuals formed relationships that crossed class lines. For instance, powerful men might take slave women or freedwomen as mistresses or concubines. A few even married these women, which could cause gossip or scorn among the elite but was not entirely unheard of. Genuine love could arise, but critics sometimes claimed that the man was being manipulated or that the woman was just seeking social advancement. Still, numerous personal letters, inscriptions, and epitaphs show heartfelt devotion in such unions, hinting that love could bridge social gaps, even if the broader society looked down on it.

Parental Love and Children

Children were very important to Romans. They carried on the family name and ensured that religious rituals and ancestral worship continued. Parents were expected to love their children, raise them properly, and teach them Roman values. Fathers held formal authority (*patria potestas*), yet mothers often spent more time with children during their early years. Wealthy families might hire tutors or send sons to a grammaticus (teacher) for further education.

Roman art sometimes depicted children with their parents, showing scenes of domestic life that suggest warmth and affection. Tomb inscriptions and epitaphs for deceased children can be very emotional, revealing deep parental grief. Death rates were high in the ancient world, so losing a child was a common tragedy. In these inscriptions, fathers and mothers expressed genuine sadness, underscoring the strong emotional bonds that existed despite the formalities of Roman family structure.

Friendship and Comradeship

Besides romantic love and familial bonds, Romans placed high value on *amicitia* (friendship). This was often tied to social and political networking. A friendship could involve exchanging favors, supporting each other in business or politics, and offering loyalty in times of need. While some friendships were purely utilitarian, deeper bonds could form as well.

Letters from authors like **Cicero** show that friendship could blend personal affection with mutual benefit. Cicero wrote lovingly to close friends, praising their character and lamenting their absence. These friendships sometimes became crucial in Roman politics, where alliances could shift rapidly. A friend's betrayal was seen as a grave moral failing. In a culture that prized honor and loyalty, a strong friendship was akin to a form of love—valued for trust and commitment, not just personal gain.

Public Displays of Affection and Entertainment

In the public sphere, especially in the city of Rome itself, life was busy and often chaotic. Large gatherings took place at the Forum for business or politics, while the Circus Maximus and the Colosseum hosted races and gladiatorial games. Couples might attend these events together, although women of high status were expected to show modesty and remain discreet. Public displays of affection were not the norm for respectable people. However, men of lower status, or younger couples who were less bound by etiquette, may have been more open in showing affection.

Theater performances and public festivals sometimes included romantic storylines or comedic sketches about love. The Roman audience loved drama, whether tragic or humorous. Even in these crowded venues, love and relationship themes were popular because they reflected everyday desires and conflicts. Gladiatorial games, though violent, also had a social aspect where people mingled, formed bonds, and perhaps even found romantic connections in the stands.

Slavery and Emotional Bonds

A large part of Rome's population were slaves. They had no legal rights, and their relationships were not recognized as official marriages. Yet slaves formed deep emotional bonds, both with each other and sometimes with their owners. Some masters freed a slave they loved, making that person a freedman or freedwoman, and then married them. While such cases might have caused controversy, they highlight that love could transcend legal status.

Enslaved people might be forced into sexual relationships or separated from loved ones if sold away, reflecting a harsh reality where love and emotional attachments could be shattered. Letters and documents reveal the heartbreak of such separations. Yet it was also possible for a kind master to grant manumission (freedom) to a loyal slave, showing that personal affection sometimes overcame the profit motive or social norms. Even so, the power imbalance meant that love involving slaves was rarely an equal relationship.

Religious Influences on Love and Marriage

Traditional Roman religion had gods like Juno (associated with marriage) and Venus (associated with love and desire). Families performed household rituals to honor protective spirits, called *Lares* and *Penates*. These religious practices generally supported family unity and stability, creating an atmosphere where marriage was seen as blessed by the gods. Sacrifices and prayers were offered to ensure a harmonious home and healthy children.

In the later Republic and Empire, foreign cults spread into Rome. The worship of Isis from Egypt or Cybele from Asia Minor attracted followers, some of whom valued themes of fertility, rebirth, and divine love. Mystery cults offered emotional and personal experiences with the deity, sometimes giving believers a feeling of closeness or spiritual union. Though not everyone embraced these cults, they introduced new ideas about devotion, possibly influencing how some Romans thought about love as more than just duty or pleasure.

Expressions of Love in Epitaphs and Monuments

One way we see genuine expressions of love is through epitaphs on tombstones. Many surviving inscriptions describe a beloved wife or husband in touching language. A typical inscription might say, "To the sweetest wife, who lived with me for 20 years without quarrel," or "To my husband, most loving and kind, who cared for our children well." These brief lines, chiseled in stone, indicate that real affection and companionship were treasured and remembered. The fact that people spent money on monuments and inscriptions for their spouses and children shows that love was important enough to memorialize publicly.

Some elaborate tombs displayed sculptures of the couple standing side by side, sometimes holding hands or with arms around each other's shoulders. Such images mirrored earlier Etruscan funerary art, which also showed couples together in the afterlife. Romans believed in preserving the memory of the deceased. By depicting themselves as loving partners, they declared to future generations the bond they shared in life.

Love During the Late Republic and Early Empire

The transition from the Roman Republic to the Empire, under Augustus, brought changes in laws and social attitudes. Augustus enacted the **Lex Julia** and the **Lex**

Papia Poppaea, aimed at encouraging marriage and childbearing among the elite. These laws also penalized adultery, trying to uphold a traditional moral code. Some families complied, but others found ways around the rules. Love affairs, political scandals, and divorces remained part of Roman high society.

Writers from this era often criticized hypocrisy. For example, the poet Juvenal wrote satires about social and moral decay. He mocked wives who cheated on traveling husbands and husbands who were too controlling. His biting verses suggest that, while Augustus might have hoped to restore family values, the reality of love and marriage in Rome was complex, with many private desires chafing under public regulations.

Military Life and Love

Rome was known for its powerful legions. Soldiers were stationed throughout the empire, sometimes far from home for years. Before certain reforms, legionaries were officially prohibited from legal marriage during their service (especially in the early Principate period), though they often formed relationships or unofficial marriages with local women. Once a soldier's service ended and he returned home, or if he was granted permission to marry, he might formally recognize his children from such unions.

This separation could strain relationships, but it also led to love letters crossing great distances. Archaeologists have found writing tablets with soldiers sending greetings to wives, family, or sweethearts, wishing for good health and longing for home. These letters show the simple, heartfelt side of Roman love that persisted despite strict military rules or political conflict.

Influence on the Provinces and Beyond

As Rome expanded, it spread certain marriage practices and legal concepts to its provinces. Local peoples in Gaul, Britain, or Syria sometimes adopted Roman laws for inheritance or citizenship. Mixed marriages between Romans and locals increased, particularly when Roman colonies were founded. Over time, local gods merged with Roman gods, and local elites began to style themselves after Roman aristocrats, wearing Roman togas and building villas that included Roman-style family spaces.

Yet the flow of influence was not one-way. Romans themselves adopted local customs in various provinces. For example, in Egypt (now under Roman rule after Cleopatra's defeat), many Romans took part in Egyptian religious practices. Some married local women who brought Egyptian marriage traditions into the relationship. Love and family life in these blended communities could have unique features, drawing on both Roman law and local belief systems.

CHAPTER 8

LOVE IN EARLY CHRISTIANITY

The rise of Christianity during the late Roman Empire brought new perspectives on love, relationships, and family life. Initially, Christianity was a small movement within the diverse religious landscape of the Roman world. Over the first few centuries CE, it grew in followers despite periods of persecution. By the time Emperor Constantine embraced Christianity in the early 4th century, the faith had spread widely. Early Christian teachings introduced ideas about love that were both continuous with ancient Jewish traditions and shaped by a new focus on Jesus' message of compassion, humility, and spiritual devotion.

In this chapter, we will explore how early Christians understood love. We will also look at Christian views on marriage, the role of celibacy, the influence of church leaders, and the tension between Roman law and Christian moral teachings. While our main focus is on the first few centuries of Christianity, we will also note how these ideas laid the groundwork for later Christian concepts of love in medieval Europe and beyond.

Foundations in Jewish Tradition

Christianity emerged from a Jewish context in the province of Judea. Jesus of Nazareth and his earliest followers were Jewish, and they saw themselves as fulfilling Jewish prophecies. Jewish law and tradition already placed importance on family, marriage, and the covenant relationship with God. The Hebrew Bible taught commandments such as "Love your neighbor as yourself" (Leviticus 19:18), which Jesus reaffirmed and emphasized in his teachings.

Early Christians inherited many Jewish values about love and marriage. However, they also began to see Jesus as the ultimate example of sacrificial love, especially through the events of his crucifixion and resurrection. This focus on self-giving and compassion became central to the Christian idea of love, often referred to by the Greek term **agape**—a form of love that is selfless, merciful, and oriented toward the well-being of others. While earlier Greek culture recognized agape, Christianity turned it into a defining spiritual concept, suggesting it came directly from God's love for humanity.

Teachings of Jesus and the Apostles on Love

The Gospels and other New Testament writings contain key teachings that shaped early Christian attitudes:

1. **The Great Commandment**: Jesus said the greatest commandments were to love God with all one's heart and to love one's neighbor as oneself (Mark 12:29-31; Matthew 22:37-39). These words made love the core of Christian ethics.
2. **Sermon on the Mount**: Jesus' sermon (Matthew 5-7) spoke about loving enemies, turning the other cheek, and forgiving others. This radical call to compassion challenged the standard practices of revenge or strict justice.
3. **Marriage and Fidelity**: Jesus spoke about marriage as a bond meant to be permanent. The Gospels suggest he disapproved of casual divorce, implying that marriage should be taken seriously (Mark 10:2-12; Matthew 19:3-9).
4. **Writings of Paul**: The Apostle Paul's letters to early Christian communities frequently discuss love. In 1 Corinthians 13, he describes love as patient, kind, and enduring. While he addresses many practical issues—such as sexual morality, marriage, and community life—he emphasizes that love is the highest virtue, surpassing knowledge, prophecy, or even faith in importance.

These teachings set Christianity apart from many traditional Roman attitudes, especially those that allowed for easy divorce or saw marriage mostly as a family alliance. While early Christians still navigated Roman laws, they tried to live out these new moral teachings, often forming tight-knit communities marked by mutual care.

Christian Communities and Mutual Support

Early Christians gathered in house churches or small community groups. They practiced shared meals, prayer, and the celebration of the Eucharist (commonly understood as a commemorative meal of bread and wine in honor of Jesus). Many of the letters in the New Testament emphasize caring for the poor, widows, and orphans. This communal emphasis on charity was a practical expression of agape. It also served as a powerful draw for new converts, who witnessed a different form of social bond than what was typical in the wider Roman world.

In these communities, believers were encouraged to address one another as "brothers" and "sisters," reflecting a spiritual family united by faith, not just bloodline. This spiritual family did not replace biological families, but it sometimes competed with them. If a new Christian convert came from a non-Christian household, tensions might arise. Christian love in these groups meant prioritizing devotion to God and to fellow believers, which could conflict with traditional loyalties.

Attitudes Toward Marriage and Celibacy

Early Christians held a range of views about marriage:

1. **Marriage as Good and Holy**: Many believers followed Jewish tradition and saw marriage as instituted by God for companionship and procreation. They cited scriptures that portrayed God blessing the union of husband and wife.
2. **Celibacy and Virginity as Ideals**: Some Christians—especially leaders like Paul—suggested that celibacy could be spiritually advantageous. Paul wrote in 1 Corinthians 7 that unmarried individuals could dedicate themselves more fully to God, free from worldly distractions. Over time, the ideal of the virgin or the celibate monk or nun grew stronger in Christian thought, shaping monastic movements.
3. **Marriage as a Symbol of Christ and the Church**: Writings such as Ephesians 5:21-33 compared marriage to the relationship between Christ and the Church. The husband's love for his wife was likened to Christ's sacrificial love for believers. This imagery elevated marriage to a sacred sign of divine love, even as celibacy was also praised.

Initially, these views were not formalized into a single doctrine. Different church communities balanced them in various ways. Some leaders encouraged young Christians to marry and raise faithful children. Others urged believers to consider celibacy or ascetic practices. These differences often sparked debates. However, what united them was the emphasis on holiness and commitment in relationships, rather than viewing marriage as just a family alliance or a property exchange.

Changing Family Norms

The spread of Christianity introduced new challenges to Roman familial expectations. For instance, a young Roman woman who converted to

Christianity might resist an arranged marriage if her intended husband was a pagan. Alternatively, a Christian man might insist on monogamous fidelity in a culture where men often took concubines or had affairs with slaves. Over time, Christian teaching placed greater moral weight on the marriage bond, influencing the Roman concept of conjugal life.

As Christianity gained legal status, especially after Emperor Constantine's Edict of Milan (313 CE), Christians could openly practice their faith. Church leaders began advising imperial authorities on moral and legal matters. Gradually, certain Christian ideals about marriage and chastity filtered into Roman law. For example, Emperor Theodosius I (late 4th century) made Christianity the state religion, which led to more direct influence of Christian leaders on marriage and family policies.

Love Feasts and Communal Care

Besides the Eucharist, some Christian groups practiced what were called **agape feasts**—communal meals to symbolize unity and mutual support. People shared food, prayed together, and sometimes read from scripture. These gatherings likely strengthened the sense that love (agape) was not just an inner feeling but an active care for the well-being of others.

The emphasis on charity also shaped the way Christians responded to crises. When plagues or famines struck, Christians gained a reputation for nursing the sick or feeding the hungry—whether or not those in need were believers. Such actions were viewed as an outpouring of divine love. Over time, institutions like hospitals and hostels for travelers developed, reflecting the idea that Christian love should be practical and inclusive.

Martyrdom and Sacrificial Love

In the first few centuries, Roman authorities sometimes persecuted Christians, suspecting them of disloyalty to the empire because Christians refused to worship the Roman gods or the emperor's divinity. In this tense environment, some believers were arrested and faced trials, torture, or execution. Martyrdom was seen as the ultimate act of faith and love for God, since martyrs chose to remain loyal to Christ's teachings even at the cost of their lives.

Stories of martyrs like Perpetua and Felicitas in Carthage (3rd century CE) show deep bonds of love within Christian communities. Perpetua was a young mother who, along with her servant Felicitas, chose to die rather than renounce her faith. Their story highlights both spiritual love for God and mutual love among believers. Christians admired such courage, and the memory of martyrs became a source of inspiration. The idea of sacrificing one's life out of devotion influenced how early Christians talked about love—as something more powerful than fear or pain.

Influence of Greek Thought on Christian Love

While Christianity drew heavily from Jewish scriptures, it also operated in a world shaped by Greek philosophy. Early Christian thinkers, such as **Clement of Alexandria** and **Origen**, studied Platonic and Stoic ideas. They attempted to reconcile them with Christian teachings. For example, the notion of controlling one's passions, which Stoics had taught, fit well with Christian calls for chastity and moderation. The idea of rising from physical desire to spiritual love found echoes in the Christian journey from earthly attachments to divine fellowship.

At the same time, Christian doctrine introduced the figure of Christ as the incarnation of God's love, emphasizing humility and forgiveness. This concept was different from the classical Greek ideal of a distant, supreme "Form of Good" (as in Plato) or the Stoic notion of a rational divine order. To Christians, God personally reached out in love through Jesus. This made love an active, relational power at the heart of the cosmos, rather than an abstract principle or purely moral virtue. Early Christian sermons, letters, and prayers are filled with references to God's boundless love (agape) as the source and model for all human affection.

Role of Church Leaders and Councils

As the Church became more organized, bishops and councils started to shape official positions on marriage and sexuality. Although detailed church laws (canon law) would develop more fully in the medieval period, seeds were planted early on. Church leaders taught that marriage was a sacred union, blessed by God, which should reflect Christ's faithful love. Divorce became increasingly frowned upon, and remarriage after divorce was debated. Some leaders, like the Bishop of Rome (later recognized as the Pope), wielded growing authority, and their statements influenced Christian communities widely.

The **Council of Elvira** (early 4th century) in Spain, for example, had canons (rules) condemning adultery and setting conditions for penance. Later councils in other regions passed similar rulings, suggesting that Christians saw sexual sin as serious but still believed in the possibility of repentance. Over time, these official decisions helped form a moral framework around love, marriage, and family life that contrasted with some looser Roman customs.

Ascetic Movements and Monastic Love

Not all Christians chose marriage. Many were drawn to ascetic movements that emphasized celibacy, prayer, and renunciation of worldly possessions. Hermits in the Egyptian desert, such as **Anthony the Great** (3rd–4th century), sought spiritual union with God through solitude. Monastic communities emerged, where men (monks) and women (nuns) dedicated themselves to chastity, communal living, and constant worship. They saw their life as a higher calling, an expression of total love for God without the distractions of marriage or family responsibilities.

These ascetics and monastics practiced mutual support within their communities, calling each other "brother" or "sister." Love within these groups aimed to reflect divine love, focusing on humility, service, and shared devotion. While this might seem far from romantic love, it still presented a form of deep emotional bond and loyalty—just in a different context. Over time, monasticism would become very influential in Christian history, shaping ideas about holiness and love as spiritual dedication rather than worldly passion.

Christian Love Versus Pagan Society

As Christianity spread, it often clashed with pagan culture. Traditional Roman society had included many gods, festivals, and practices that Christians began rejecting. Where pagans might view the emperor as semi-divine and perform public sacrifices, Christians insisted that worship belonged to God alone. This refusal to participate in state religious rites sometimes led to accusations that Christians were unpatriotic.

Also, the moral teachings about strict marital fidelity or celibacy conflicted with the more permissive Roman attitudes. While many Romans respected strong family values, they also tolerated affairs, prostitution, and other behaviors that Christian leaders condemned as sinful. Christian emphasis on charity toward the poor and slaves was another contrast. Though this charity did not always challenge the social hierarchy directly, it did suggest a different set of priorities—loving service rather than displays of wealth or power.

Literary Expressions of Early Christian Love

Unlike classical Latin literature, which celebrated romantic adventures (as in Ovid) or personal passion (as in Catullus), early Christian writings centered on spiritual love, moral guidance, and community-building. The *Acts of the Apostles* and the letters of Paul, Peter, and John in the New Testament gave examples of believers caring for each other across cultural divides. Other authors, like the **Apostolic Fathers** (Clement of Rome, Ignatius of Antioch, Polycarp, etc.) and later church fathers (such as Augustine in the late 4th and early 5th century), continued to teach that love was the highest Christian virtue.

St. Augustine, in his works such as *Confessions* and *On Christian Doctrine*, reflected on human love, sin, and divine grace. He admitted his own youthful pursuits of passion before converting to Christianity, then spoke of how true fulfillment lay in loving God wholeheartedly. Augustine's personal journey showed that Christians could still experience human desire but aimed to transform it into a higher love aligned with God's will.

The Changing Legal Landscape

After Constantine legalized Christianity, Emperor Theodosius made it the official state religion near the end of the 4th century. Over time, Church leaders advised emperors on moral laws. Gradually, Roman law began to reflect Christian values:

- **Restrictions on divorce** became stricter, emphasizing the permanence of marriage.

- **Adultery** was still punishable, now sometimes with the Church's involvement in judging moral offenses.

- **Infanticide**, which had existed in pagan Rome, was increasingly condemned. Christians encouraged the care of unwanted children, sometimes founding institutions to house orphans.

While the empire's legal system was slow to fully change, we see a gradual shift toward ideals of marriage as a lifetime commitment, shaped by mutual love and overseen by ecclesiastical (church) authority. Still, these changes were not uniform across all regions of the empire. Local customs, personal wealth, and social class continued to matter. But the guiding moral principles had begun to shift in favor of Christian teachings about faithfulness, charity, and the sacredness of marriage.

Pilgrimage and Sacred Devotion

Another way Christians expressed love was through pilgrimage. Believers traveled to holy sites—like Jerusalem, the place of Jesus' crucifixion and resurrection; Rome, where the apostles Peter and Paul were said to be martyred; or local shrines dedicated to saints. These journeys symbolized both devotion to God and communal solidarity with fellow pilgrims. Along the way, they formed friendships, shared resources, and prayed together, strengthening bonds of spiritual love.

Pilgrims often returned with relics or stories of miracles, inspiring others to make the same journey. Such acts of devotion showed that Christian love went beyond private relationships—it extended to the entire community of believers, living and dead. Visiting a martyr's tomb or a sacred site became an act of love and gratitude, reinforcing the connection between individual faith and the broader church.

Love and the Cult of Saints

As the cult of saints developed, believers formed emotional attachments to holy men and women who were believed to intercede before God on behalf of the living. People prayed to saints, wrote about their miracles, and held feast days to celebrate them. This practice created a sense of intimate spiritual friendship across the boundaries of life and death. The love believers felt for saints, and the saints' supposed love for humankind, offered comfort and a sense of closeness to the divine.

Relics—physical remains or items associated with saints—were treated with reverence. Churches that housed important relics became pilgrimage destinations. While some skeptics questioned the authenticity of certain relics, the emotional significance for many Christians was profound. The veneration of saints was seen as a reflection of the powerful love that united the entire "body of Christ," meaning all believers across time and space.

Tensions Within the Christian Community

Although early Christians prided themselves on love and unity, disagreements arose. Different bishops might argue about doctrine, such as the nature of Christ (leading to councils like Nicaea in 325 CE and Chalcedon in 451 CE). Rival groups, labeled heretics, formed their own interpretations of scripture. A famous example is **Donatism** in North Africa, where believers questioned whether sacraments performed by priests who had sinned were valid. These disputes sometimes led to hostility, showing that Christians struggled to practice the same love they preached.

Additionally, not all Christians embraced the same attitudes toward marriage. Some extremist ascetic groups claimed that total sexual abstinence was necessary, even within marriage. More moderate voices insisted marriage was blessed by God. Church councils tried to set guidelines, but local variations remained. Despite these internal conflicts, the ideal of love as central to Christian identity endured.

Enduring Impact on Future Societies

Early Christian notions of love laid the groundwork for much of medieval and later Christian thought. The idea that marriage should be a sacred bond—reflecting Christ's love—would later develop into the full sacramental understanding of marriage in the Catholic Church. The emphasis on charity influenced monastic orders and church-led charitable institutions, which provided for the poor, the sick, and travelers well into the Middle Ages. The concept of a spiritual family of believers shaped how people understood community and social responsibility.

Eventually, Christian love also intersected with the idea of chivalry in medieval Europe, blending spiritual devotion and romantic ideals in the concept of "courtly love." But that is a later development. In the early centuries, Christianity's fresh focus on agape (selfless, divine love) already marked a significant shift from the more pragmatic or status-driven relationships of the Roman world. While Roman cultural patterns did not vanish overnight, the Christian message about compassion, fidelity, and spiritual unity left a lasting mark on Western ideas about love.

CHAPTER 9

LOVE IN THE ISLAMIC GOLDEN AGE

The "Islamic Golden Age" is a term often used to describe a broad period in Islamic history, usually spanning from the 8th century to roughly the mid-13th century. During this time, the Islamic world experienced a flourishing of art, science, philosophy, and literature. Powerful dynasties like the Abbasids in Baghdad, the Umayyads in Al-Andalus (Muslim Spain), and others presided over a vast empire that stretched from North Africa and the Middle East to parts of Central Asia and even into the Iberian Peninsula. People from diverse backgrounds—Arabs, Persians, Turks, Berbers, and more—contributed to a rich cultural tapestry.

Love during this era was shaped by the teachings of Islam and by local customs. Islamic scholars wrote treatises on marriage and family, while poets and mystics produced verses that celebrated both human and divine love. The concept of love had many layers: it could be spiritual, romantic, poetic, or tied to marriage and family life. In this chapter, we will explore the cultural, religious, and philosophical aspects of love in the Islamic Golden Age, looking at marriage customs, poetic traditions, Sufi mysticism, and the daily experiences of ordinary people.

1. THE RELIGIOUS AND CULTURAL CONTEXT

1.1 The Teachings of Islam on Love and Marriage
Islamic teachings about love and marriage are found primarily in the Quran (the holy book of Islam) and the Hadith (reports of the Prophet Muhammad's words and actions). Marriage is highly valued in Islam, seen as a legal contract (*nikah*) as well as a moral safeguard and a source of mutual affection and mercy. The Quran often describes the marital bond as being based on tranquility, love (*mawadda*), and compassion (*rahma*). While arranged marriages were common—similar to other cultures of the time—Islamic law placed some emphasis on mutual consent. Both the bride and groom should agree to the union, although in practice, family influence was strong.

Love in Islam also includes broader concepts of compassion and brotherly love among believers. The Prophet Muhammad taught kindness, mercy, and mutual help. This shaped social norms around charity and communal care. While romantic love between spouses was recognized as important, love for neighbors, the poor, or travelers was also celebrated.

1.2 The Caliphate and Its Influence

The Abbasid caliphate in Baghdad (beginning in 750 CE) fostered a culture of learning and literature. Scholars translated works of philosophy and science from Greek, Persian, and other languages, creating an atmosphere of intellectual curiosity. Within this environment, discussions of love, ethics, and family life mixed with debates on theology and law. The royal courts, especially in cities like Baghdad and Córdoba, sponsored poets and artists who explored themes of devotion and longing. As the empire expanded, these cultural ideas spread across a wide region, influencing love poetry, music, and social customs.

2. COURTSHIP, MARRIAGE, AND FAMILY

2.1 Arranged Marriages and Family Roles

Like many societies of the time, marriages in the Islamic world were often arranged by families. The groom's family and the bride's family would negotiate a marriage contract, which included the *mahr* (a mandatory gift from the groom to the bride, sometimes paid immediately and sometimes deferred). The *mahr* could be money, land, or even an item of special value. The bride's consent was generally required, though parental influence could be strong.

Families placed importance on lineage, reputation, and piety when selecting a match. Among the elites, marriages helped build political alliances or reinforce social status. Among ordinary people, the goal was stability, shared labor, and raising a family. While we might see this as a practical approach, love and affection were still valued within these marriages. Many couples formed strong bonds, supported by teachings that stressed harmony and mutual respect.

2.2 Wedding Customs

Wedding celebrations varied by region but often included reciting the marriage contract in front of witnesses, offering gifts, and organizing feasts. Wealthy families hosted elaborate celebrations with music, dancing, and decorated venues. Poets might be invited to compose verses for the occasion, praising the couple and their families. In the royal courts, lavish ceremonies could last for days, with guests from far-flung regions. Even simpler village weddings typically involved communal gatherings, shared meals, and blessings for the new couple.

2.3 Polygamy and Its Regulations

Islamic law allows a man to have up to four wives, provided he treats them all fairly. This practice is known as polygamy. However, not all men chose or could afford multiple wives. Maintaining multiple households required significant resources, and many men simply did not have the means. Among royalty or wealthy families, polygamy sometimes helped forge political ties. Still, there were guidelines meant to ensure that each wife had legal and financial rights, though in practice, disputes and favoritism could arise.

3. LITERARY AND POETIC TRADITIONS

3.1 Arabic Love Poetry

One of the brightest parts of the Islamic Golden Age is its poetry, including love poems that expressed deep feelings and longing. Pre-Islamic Arabic poetry had already established the tradition of the *qasida* (ode), which often began with the poet lamenting the loss or absence of a beloved. With the expansion of the Islamic empire and the blending of cultures, new styles emerged. Many poems focused on courtly love—sometimes idealized, sometimes playful.

A famous example is **Ibn Hazm** of Al-Andalus, who wrote *The Ring of the Dove* in the 11th century. This treatise explored the nature of love, describing its signs and stages. Drawing upon personal experience and anecdotal stories, Ibn Hazm combined observations on human psychology with poetic language. This work remains a key text for understanding how love was conceptualized in the medieval Islamic world, emphasizing both the joy and the pain that love can bring.

3.2 Persian Influences

As the Islamic empire expanded into Persia (Iran), Persian literary traditions blended with Arabic forms. Persian poets wrote works that combined Islamic themes with older Persian motifs. Court poets, like **Rudaki**, performed for rulers and aristocrats, praising their patrons but also including romantic or philosophical reflections in their verses. Over time, Persian became a major literary language in the eastern parts of the Islamic world.

Poets like **Ferdowsi** composed the *Shahnameh* (the Book of Kings), a grand epic that included heroic tales and love stories, though it focused more on legendary kings. Others, such as **Nizami Ganjavi**, wrote narrative poems filled with romantic plots, like *Layla and Majnun*—a tragic love story that became a classic across many cultures. Though Nizami lived slightly after what some call the "peak" of the Golden Age, his work grew out of the literary environment that the earlier centuries had established.

3.3 Courtly Love and Themes of Longing

In royal courts, especially under the Abbasids or in Al-Andalus, poetry often celebrated unrequited or idealized love. Poets would describe the beloved's beauty using metaphors about nature—comparing eyes to gazelles or describing hair as dark as night. They spoke of sleepless nights, tearful longing, and the sweetness of simply gazing upon the beloved. This style influenced later European poetry, as ideas flowed from Al-Andalus into Christian parts of Spain and beyond.

While some poems addressed the love between a man and a woman, others hinted at male-male affection, especially in courtly settings. Such verses sometimes used ambiguous language, focusing on beauty and desire in ways that could be interpreted in multiple ways. This did not always reflect social realities straightforwardly; rather, it was part of a literary tradition that emphasized aesthetic appreciation and refined expression.

4. SUFISM AND SPIRITUAL LOVE

4.1 The Emergence of Sufism

Sufism is an Islamic mystical tradition that emerged in the early centuries of Islam, growing stronger around the 9th and 10th centuries. Sufis sought a direct, personal experience of the divine, emphasizing the inner path of spirituality. Love is a key concept in Sufi thought, often described as the force that draws the believer closer to God. While Islamic law (*sharia*) governs external actions, Sufis focused on the inner relationship (*tariqa*) between the individual soul and God. They often used the language of earthly love as a metaphor for divine love.

4.2 Key Sufi Poets and Their Expressions of Love

Some of the best-known Sufi poets lived a bit later (for example, Jalaluddin Rumi in the 13th century), but their roots trace back to the Golden Age of Islamic civilization. Rumi wrote famously about longing for God, describing this longing in terms of separation from the Beloved—using the imagery of earthly desire to hint at spiritual union. Earlier Sufis, like Rabia al-Adawiyya (8th century), expressed a pure, selfless love for God, rejecting the idea of worship for reward or fear of punishment. She said she worshiped God out of love alone. Her poems and sayings spoke of a relationship so intense that it eclipsed all worldly attachments.

4.3 The Concept of Divine Love

In Sufism, the love between a man and a woman can serve as a reflection of, or stepping stone to, a higher, divine love. Sufi teachers used romantic symbolism—like the moth drawn to a flame—to illustrate the soul's yearning to be united with God. This mystical approach did not reject earthly love but placed it within a larger spiritual framework. Hence, poems that might look simply romantic often carry deeper meanings about the quest for divine truth.

Sufis also practiced ritual gatherings called *sama*, involving music, poetry, and sometimes dance (like the whirling dervishes). These sessions aimed to awaken love in the heart, removing the ego and drawing the devotee closer to God. While some conservative scholars criticized these practices, many communities embraced them. Sufism, with its focus on love, became a popular form of devotion across the Islamic world, influencing music, literature, and daily spiritual practices.

5. SOCIAL REALITIES AND DAILY LIFE

5.1 Love Across Social Classes

Within the Islamic empire, there were distinct social classes—rulers, bureaucrats, soldiers, merchants, farmers, and slaves. Upper-class families had arranged marriages that served political or economic goals, but emotional bonds could still grow. In contrast, ordinary people in towns and villages often married within their community, focusing on mutual support and shared labor. Emotional expressions of love would vary, but the broad Islamic principles of kindness and mercy provided a backdrop that encouraged caring family relationships.

Slavery existed in the Islamic world, although it had its own rules. Enslaved people could sometimes buy their freedom or be freed by their owners, and a male owner might marry a female slave (or have concubines). Emotional attachments developed in such contexts, though the power imbalance was clear. Some enslaved individuals rose to significant status, like the female slaves who became wives of rulers, influencing politics and culture—an example is Shaghab, the mother of the Abbasid Caliph al-Muqtadir, who exercised political power behind the scenes.

5.2 Gender Roles and Women's Influence

Women in the Islamic Golden Age had varying degrees of autonomy depending on family background, location, and local customs. In some urban centers like

Córdoba or Baghdad, elite women received education at home and could be patrons of the arts. Female poets like Wallada bint al-Mustakfi in Al-Andalus wrote openly about love, challenging social norms. Noblewomen sometimes owned property, ran businesses, or influenced court politics. However, many women lived more restricted lives, expected to focus on family and domestic tasks. Veiling and seclusion (in line with the practice of *purdah* in some places) limited direct public participation.

Despite these constraints, certain women had strong roles as mothers, educators, or managers of family property. Love between husband and wife might not always be displayed in public, but behind closed doors, letters and personal accounts suggest genuine affection. Parents' love for their children was also strong, with many treatises advising on the moral and religious upbringing of sons and daughters.

6. LITERARY SALONS, MUSIC, AND PERFORMANCE

6.1 Courtly Circles and Intellectual Gatherings

In major cities, wealthy patrons hosted literary salons where poets, musicians, and scholars gathered to share their work. Such gatherings provided a space for refined conversation, flirtation, and the recitation of romantic poetry. Men and women might attend, depending on local custom. In Al-Andalus, some gatherings were relatively mixed, with learned women participating. In the East, gatherings might be more male-dominated, though women sometimes held their own private sessions.

6.2 Music and Song

Music was an important medium for expressing love. Skilled musicians composed songs about longing, separation, and the sweetness of union. Lute players, singers, and composers were highly respected, especially in cities like Baghdad, Damascus, or Córdoba. The music of the time included influences from Persian, Arabic, Greek, and other traditions, creating a rich fusion. Singers like Ibrahim al-Mawsili or Ziryab (a notable figure in Al-Andalus) were known not just for their musical talent but for bringing new styles and tastes to the courts. Love songs were part of their repertoire, capturing the hearts of listeners and possibly shaping how people talked about affection.

7. PHILOSOPHICAL AND ETHICAL VIEWS ON LOVE

7.1 Islamic Law (Fiqh) and Moral Guidelines
Islamic jurisprudence (fiqh) addressed marriage, divorce, custody of children, and related matters. Love itself was not a primary legal category, but the underlying principles—mercy, compassion, fairness—were embedded in the law. Scholars debated details, such as the rights of wives to divorce if not properly cared for, or how a husband should treat his wives if polygamy was practiced. These legal arguments showed that, while not always focusing on "romantic love," early Islamic law tried to ensure mutual respect and well-being within marriage.

7.2 Philosophical Writings
Philosophers like **Al-Kindi, Al-Farabi,** and **Ibn Sina (Avicenna)** engaged with Greek philosophy. They studied Plato, Aristotle, and others, including their ideas on love. Avicenna wrote about the soul's longing for the ultimate Good—close to the concept of divine love in Sufism. Some philosophers wrote treatises on the psychology of love, analyzing it as a force that moves the soul. While these works were more abstract, they influenced the intellectual class's view of love, bridging religion, reason, and emotional experience.

7.3 Ethical Poetry and Adab Literature
Beyond romantic or Sufi poetry, there was also **adab** literature—a broad genre that included moral stories, wisdom, and etiquette. Compilations like **"Kalila wa Dimna"** (translated from earlier Indian fables) included lessons about relationships, loyalty, and betrayal. Though not always labeled as love stories, they carried moral messages about how people should treat each other with kindness, trust, and respect. Authors like **Al-Jahiz** wrote essays and treatises on social behavior, sometimes touching on love's role in forming friendships or strengthening familial bonds.

8. CROSS-CULTURAL EXCHANGES

8.1 Contacts with Byzantine and Other Empires
During the Golden Age, the Islamic world maintained diplomatic, commercial, and cultural contacts with the Byzantine Empire, various European regions, India, and beyond. Translations of texts and the movement of merchants, scholars, and travelers led to an exchange of ideas. Concepts of courtly love may

have flowed back and forth, with Islamic poets influencing European troubadours, especially across the frontier in Al-Andalus and the Crusader States in the Levant.

8.2 Jewish and Christian Minorities
Within Islamic lands, there were significant Jewish and Christian communities. They spoke Arabic or local languages, contributed to arts and sciences, and sometimes participated in government. Jewish scholars, like those in Andalusian cities, wrote poetry in Hebrew that echoed Arabic love poetry. Christian communities adapted to Islamic rule, and in some places, there was a blending of cultural elements. While religious boundaries remained, the shared language (Arabic) and intellectual pursuits created overlapping literary traditions. This environment fostered many viewpoints on love, from the purely religious to the deeply romantic.

9. CHALLENGES AND CRITIQUES

9.1 Conservative Reactions
Not everyone in the Islamic world approved of the open discussion of romantic desire or the extravagant gatherings at court. Conservative scholars often warned against letting passion overshadow one's devotion to God. They criticized love poetry that seemed too sensual or gatherings that encouraged flirtation. Over time, different regions had different levels of strictness. Some courts tolerated and even promoted free expression in poetry, while others imposed more conservative rules.

9.2 Social and Political Upheaval
The Islamic Golden Age was not without conflict. Factional disputes, rebellions, and external threats sometimes disrupted life. The Mongol invasions in the 13th century, for example, led to the sack of Baghdad in 1258, effectively ending the Abbasid Caliphate. Such upheavals impacted patronage for the arts. Poets might lose their sponsors or flee warfare. In some areas, intellectual and artistic life continued under new rulers, but in others, it declined.

9.3 Women's Literary Voices
While a few female poets made their mark, most women's voices were less recorded or preserved. This means our understanding of how women in the Islamic Golden Age felt or wrote about love is limited. Nonetheless, the survival of works by figures like the Andalusian princess Wallada bint al-Mustakfi (11th century) shows that some women wrote candidly about affection and relationships, challenging traditional boundaries.

10. LEGACIES AND INFLUENCES

10.1 Impact on Later Islamic Dynasties

Even as the political landscape shifted—through the rise of new powers like the Mamluks or the Ottomans—the literary and cultural achievements of the Golden Age lived on. Sufi orders continued to spread, carrying their message of divine love. Poetic traditions persisted, with new poets building on the foundations laid by earlier masters. The Islamic concept of marriage as both a contract and an emotional bond remained central in many Muslim-majority regions.

10.2 Transmission to Medieval Europe

Trade routes and the Crusades introduced Europeans to Islamic scholarship, poetry, and possibly to some of the concepts that shaped courtly love in medieval Europe. The theme of longing and admiration from afar, central to troubadour poetry, may have roots in or parallels with Arabic love poetry. While the exact paths of influence are debated by scholars, the cultural interactions were significant. Places like Sicily and Al-Andalus were key crossroads where Muslim, Christian, and Jewish traditions mingled.

10.3 Lasting Cultural Memory

Today, many of the works from the Islamic Golden Age remain influential. The Sufi poetry of Jalaluddin Rumi, though he lived just after the "classical" Golden Age, is widely read across the world, speaking of love as a unifying force beyond religious or cultural boundaries. Stories like *Layla and Majnun* continue to inspire music, art, and literature, reflecting the timeless appeal of tragic romance. These legacies remind us that love—whether earthly, spiritual, or poetic—was a central theme in a period often celebrated for its learning and cultural achievements.

CHAPTER 10

LOVE IN MEDIEVAL EUROPE

Medieval Europe spans roughly from the 5th century to the late 15th century, beginning with the fall of the Western Roman Empire and transitioning into the early modern period. During these centuries, Europe was a patchwork of kingdoms, principalities, and feudal estates. The Catholic Church grew into a powerful institution, shaping laws, ethics, and social norms. Political and cultural changes were constant. The Carolingian dynasty, the feudal system, the Crusades, and the gradual rise of urban centers all contributed to the medieval world's complexity.

Love in Medieval Europe was influenced by religious ideals, feudal obligations, and emerging cultural movements. The bond of marriage was often arranged to secure alliances and property, yet romantic affection—expressed in literature, art, and personal letters—still found its place. The Catholic Church's teachings on marriage and morality grew increasingly central, while popular expressions of love, such as troubadour poetry and chivalric romances, introduced new themes of courtly devotion. In this chapter, we will explore how love was perceived, lived, and celebrated in Medieval Europe before turning to later developments like courtly love and the Renaissance in subsequent chapters.

1. TRANSITION FROM LATE ANTIQUITY TO THE EARLY MIDDLE AGES

1.1 The Influence of Roman and Germanic Traditions
As the Western Roman Empire collapsed in the 5th century, various Germanic tribes—such as the Franks, Visigoths, and Lombards—established kingdoms on former Roman territories. Roman law and Christian values did not disappear; instead, they merged with local customs. This blending shaped how marriages were arranged and how people understood family bonds. Among Germanic peoples, bridewealth (similar to a bride price) was common, and clan loyalties often overshadowed personal choice in marriage.

The expanding influence of the Church introduced Christian doctrines about the sanctity of marriage and the avoidance of divorce. Yet local tribal practices and older Roman customs continued to inform everyday life. In many regions, people saw marriage as a strategic tool for consolidating land and forging alliances. Romantic love might develop later within these unions, but it was rarely the main reason for getting married.

1.2 Role of the Early Medieval Church
During the early Middle Ages, the Church solidified its structure under bishops and the papacy. Clergy preached about sin, redemption, and the importance of chastity outside marriage. While the Church did not yet fully control all aspects of marriage, it encouraged practices like monogamy and frowned upon easy divorce. Marriage gradually took on a more sacred character, with church ceremonies becoming more common. Spiritual love, directed toward God and the saints, was taught to be higher than any earthly love, but that did not deny the value of marital affection.

2. FEUDAL SOCIETY AND FAMILY BONDS

2.1 Feudal Obligations and Dynastic Marriages
During the High Middle Ages, feudalism structured much of European society. Lords owned land, vassals served them in exchange for protection, and peasants worked the land. For the nobility, marriage was a tool to secure alliances and property rights. Marriages were arranged by families, often at a very young age. A noble family might offer a daughter in marriage to a powerful neighbor in exchange for military support or access to strategic lands.

Because noble families were keen to preserve wealth and titles, romantic feelings were secondary in these arrangements. But that does not mean love never emerged. In some cases, spouses developed genuine bonds of respect and affection over time. Yet it was also common for extramarital relationships, affairs, or clandestine romances to occur if the arranged marriage lacked emotional warmth.

2.2 The Concept of Household and Extended Kin
Families in medieval Europe often included extended kin—uncles, aunts, cousins—who lived together or nearby. Marriages tied not just two individuals but entire kin groups. Family honor mattered a great deal. Disputes or insults could spark feuds, so a harmonious marriage might help keep peace between

lineages. Love within this system was part loyalty, part strategic cooperation. Children were raised to uphold the family name and continue its alliances.

Among peasants, marriage could be simpler but was still influenced by local customs and economic factors. A farming family might marry their children to neighbors who had adjacent land, hoping to combine fields or share labor. The Church's insistence on monogamy, alongside local traditions, meant that peasants also followed set customs regarding courtship and union. Even so, personal attraction could play a role when deciding a match, especially among common folk who did not have massive estates to protect.

3. THE CATHOLIC CHURCH AND MARRIAGE

3.1 The Growing Role of Church Law
By the 12th century, the Church had developed a stronger, more unified legal system known as canon law. Marriage was increasingly seen as a sacrament—a sacred bond instituted by God. Church councils debated and set rules for valid marriages: mutual consent of the man and woman was required, and bigamy or incest were prohibited. A famous church decree stated that **marriage existed from the moment of mutual consent**, not just from a public ceremony. This gave some couples a chance to "secretly" exchange vows if families opposed their union, though such unions could later cause disputes.

3.2 Indissolubility of Marriage and Rare Annulments
As the Church's teachings became more standardized, marriage was treated as permanent. Divorce in the modern sense was almost impossible—one could only seek an annulment if the marriage was deemed invalid from the start (for reasons like consanguinity or lack of consent). This permanence underscored the seriousness of the marriage bond. Ideally, husbands and wives would love and support each other for life. Yet many marriages lacked emotional closeness, especially if they were arranged for dynastic reasons. Still, the Church's emphasis on mutual support and the sanctity of marriage did encourage couples to find at least some affectionate partnership.

3.3 Monastic and Clerical Views on Love
Monks and nuns followed vows of chastity, devoting themselves fully to spiritual love for God. Monastic writers, such as Bernard of Clairvaux, wrote about divine love using language that sometimes resembled romantic devotion. This approach—where the soul longs for union with God—mirrored some themes found in Islamic Sufi poetry (though the cultural contexts were different). Clerics

who were not monastic still had to follow celibacy rules (though this was enforced at varying levels throughout the Middle Ages). These teachings created a contrast between sacred, non-physical love for God and the permissible but more earthly love within marriage.

4. EMOTIONAL LIFE AND EXPRESSIONS OF LOVE

4.1 Letters and Personal Accounts

While many medieval documents are legal, religious, or administrative, some personal letters survive. These letters can reveal genuine affection between spouses, parents and children, or friends. Medieval people wrote about missing loved ones, about joy in reunion, or about grief when someone died. Historians studying these letters see that while the public face of marriage could be formal, personal feelings were still important. Some letters mention acts of kindness, like sending gifts or offering comforting words. That said, literacy was not widespread, so such letters typically come from the nobility or the clergy.

4.2 Art and Imagery

Medieval art often had religious themes, but there were also depictions of couples, families, and scenes that hinted at romantic affection. Church wall paintings, illuminated manuscripts, and tapestries could show weddings, lovers meeting in gardens, or biblical stories of marital devotion (such as Tobias and Sarah). Secular art commissioned by nobles might include small emblems of love, like hearts or flowers, in decorative margins. However, the idea of "romantic love" as a public theme was not as widespread as it would become in the later medieval era, especially with the rise of courtly love traditions.

5. CROSS-CULTURAL INFLUENCES AND THE CRUSADES

5.1 Contact with the Islamic World

From the late 11th century onward, the Crusades brought Europeans into greater contact with the Islamic East. Crusader states were established in parts of the Levant, where Western knights interacted with Byzantine and Muslim populations. Some marriages and relationships formed across religious lines, though these were not the norm. Trade and cultural exchange also grew, especially through cities like Venice or through the Reconquista in Spain. Ideas about poetry, music, and possibly certain concepts of chivalry and romantic devotion may have passed between Islamic and Christian cultures.

5.2 Influence on Literature

Some scholars argue that the tradition of European courtly love was partly inspired by Arabic love poetry found in Al-Andalus (Muslim Spain) or by contacts during the Crusades. While the exact origins are debated, it is clear that medieval Europe was not isolated. Merchants, travelers, and scholars carried new ideas across the Mediterranean. European troubadours, for example, might have absorbed motifs of longing, praise of the beloved's beauty, and the tension of unfulfilled desire—elements found in earlier Arabic poetry. Over time, these influences contributed to the shaping of new literary styles in Europe.

6. DAILY LIFE: TOWNS, VILLAGES, AND RURAL COMMUNITIES

6.1 Peasant Life and Marriage Customs

For the majority of the medieval population—peasants working on farms—love and marriage were tied to survival and cooperation. Parents arranged many matches, focusing on practical concerns like land use or the sharing of resources. However, local festivals, church feasts, and communal gatherings gave young people some chances to meet. The Church taught that both parties' consent was necessary, so a forced marriage was frowned upon. Still, social pressure could be strong. Families needed to secure reliable partners for farm work and future inheritance.

When peasants married, celebrations might include dancing, communal meals, and singing. Gifts were often modest—maybe livestock or household goods to help the new couple start their life. As in wealthier circles, the notion of romantic love might or might not be the main driver, but many couples found personal affection and mutual support as they built a household together.

6.2 Urban Centers and Merchant Families

By the High Middle Ages, some towns and cities grew, spurred by commerce, crafts, and trade guilds. Merchant families arranged marriages that consolidated wealth or joined business interests. A guild master might marry his daughter to the son of another respected merchant, ensuring business alliances. Even so, these urban environments could offer slightly more freedom in choosing a spouse than in tightly controlled noble lineages. The growth of guild culture and city life introduced new social spaces—markets, fairs, or taverns—where young men and women might interact under less direct family supervision.

7. THE ROOTS OF COURTLY LOVE

7.1 Troubadours and Minnesingers
In the late 11th and 12th centuries, a new form of love poetry arose in the Occitan language of Southern France, performed by **troubadours**. These poets celebrated the idea of **fin'amor** (refined love), which was often addressed to a noble lady who was married or otherwise unattainable. The love described was both passionate and controlled, emphasizing devotion, service, and the moral improvement of the lover through admiration of the beloved. A similar tradition appeared in German lands with the **Minnesingers**.

This poetry typically portrayed the beloved as higher in status, encouraging the lover (often a knight) to prove his worth through bravery and courtesy. While this "courtly love" was somewhat removed from the realities of medieval marriage, it became an influential literary and social code. It added a romantic layer to the relationships among nobles, providing a space where longing, admiration, and even heartbreak were elevated into art.

7.2 Courtly Love and Feudal Ideals
Historians debate whether courtly love was purely literary or reflected actual behavior among the nobility. Undoubtedly, some knights and ladies engaged in flirtations or extramarital liaisons under the influence of this new "love code." However, official marriages often remained practical. Still, courtly love shaped European thought on romantic devotion, highlighting personal longing, admiration from afar, and the idea that love could be both an inspiration and a trial.

7.3 Women in Courtly Literature
The lady at the center of a courtly love poem held great power symbolically. She was placed on a pedestal, admired from a distance. This could subvert normal social hierarchies, giving the lady moral authority over the knight. Yet, in real life, aristocratic women were usually still constrained by family duties and social limitations. The figure of the commanding lady in poems might reflect a literary ideal, not an everyday reality. Even so, certain noblewomen, like Eleanor of Aquitaine, patronized troubadours and hosted courts known for their cultivation of love poetry. This gave some women at least a measure of cultural influence.

8. RELIGIOUS LITERATURE AND MYSTICAL LOVE

8.1 Devotion to the Virgin Mary
Medieval spirituality saw a growing devotion to the Virgin Mary. Many believers viewed Mary as a compassionate, motherly figure who interceded for sinners. Artistic depictions and liturgical celebrations of Mary expanded, emphasizing qualities like mercy, purity, and tender love. In some ways, this devotion paralleled the language of courtly love, as worshipers expressed emotional reverence toward Mary. While not romantic in the literal sense, it introduced a softer, more affectionate strain into Christian piety.

8.2 Mystics and the Language of Desire
Christian mystics of the Middle Ages, such as **Hildegard of Bingen** or **Bernard of Clairvaux**, used strong emotional and even sensual language to describe the soul's union with God. Bernard's sermons on the Song of Songs likened the love between God and the soul to that of a bride and bridegroom. These texts showed that love could be intensely spiritual yet expressed in language reminiscent of human passion. Such mysticism coexisted with more formal church doctrines on marriage and chastity, highlighting a broad spectrum of how love was perceived—from the earthly to the divine.

9. SECULAR ROMANCES AND LEGENDS

9.1 The Arthurian Cycle
Legends of King Arthur and the Knights of the Round Table, popularized in works by Chrétien de Troyes and later by authors like Malory, wove together themes of chivalry, loyalty, and romantic entanglements. The famous love triangle of King Arthur, Queen Guinevere, and Sir Lancelot showcased the tension between feudal duty and passionate love. Such stories influenced the medieval imagination, suggesting that love could be a noble but dangerous force, capable of inspiring heroism or causing betrayal.

9.2 Courtly Romance Narratives
Beyond Arthurian tales, there were countless other romance narratives in French, English, German, and Italian. These stories typically involved a knight on a quest, encountering trials that tested his valor and faithfulness. The quest often centered on winning or saving a beloved, reflecting the idea that love was intertwined with moral or spiritual growth. Though these tales were fictional, they played a part in shaping how medieval audiences thought about love—encouraging ideals of devotion, perseverance, and gallantry.

10. WOMEN'S AGENCIES AND CONSTRAINTS

10.1 Noblewomen's Power
While women were largely subordinate in medieval society, some noblewomen wielded influence through family connections, land ownership, or positions as regents. Figures like **Eleanor of Aquitaine** or **Blanche of Castile** acted as patrons of the arts, founding or supporting literary courts. They could commission works praising love and virtue, thus guiding cultural tastes. Yet they still faced limitations; they were expected to marry and produce heirs, often with little say in the match.

10.2 Peasant and Townswomen
For lower-ranked women, daily life centered on labor in fields, households, or small businesses. Marriages balanced the need for labor, cooperation, and childbearing. Love might be expressed in simple ways—caring for a sick spouse, working side by side, or sharing small gifts. However, legal rights were limited, and wives often had few options if a marriage was abusive or unhappy. Some women found relative independence in towns, running shops or inns if widowed, though remarriage was common for economic stability.

11. THE EMOTIONAL CULTURE OF THE LATE MIDDLE AGES

11.1 Literature of Feeling
By the late Middle Ages (14th and 15th centuries), Europe saw more personal and introspective writings, partly influenced by changes in literacy and the growth of vernacular languages. Authors like **Geoffrey Chaucer** in England and **Christine de Pizan** in France wrote works that touched on love, marriage, and gender roles. Chaucer's *Canterbury Tales* include various perspectives on marital harmony (or lack thereof) and romantic follies. Christine de Pizan, one of the first female professional writers in Europe, argued for women's moral and intellectual capacities, challenging negative stereotypes in love and marriage.

11.2 Changing Ideals of Marriage
The late medieval Church placed stronger emphasis on a couple's free consent. Parish priests oversaw local weddings and insisted that bride and groom publicly pronounce their vows. The idea that marriage was a partnership in which love should thrive gained ground, though arranged matches did not disappear. As European economies slowly changed and some social mobility appeared, a few more individuals might have married for personal reasons. Nonetheless, family alliances, dowries, and property remained crucial throughout medieval society.

11.3 Notions of Romantic Love

The concept of romantic love as an intense personal bond continued to evolve, under the influence of courtly literature, mysticism, and changing social conditions. Yet it was still largely confined to the upper classes in a formal sense, as part of chivalric ideals. For most people, love was tied to daily survival, religious faith, and communal traditions. Even so, late medieval art and poetry reveal a growing fascination with the emotional side of love—featuring hearts, lovers in gardens, and symbolic gestures of affection.

12. IMPACT OF WAR, PLAGUE, AND CHANGE

12.1 The Hundred Years' War and Social Turmoil

Major conflicts, such as the Hundred Years' War between England and France (1337–1453), disrupted noble families and entire populations. Knights and soldiers spent long periods away from home, leaving wives to manage estates. Some romances turned bittersweet when men died in battle. Widowhood was common. Love letters and wills sometimes highlight the sorrow of separation and the responsibilities left behind. War could also break feudal marriages if alliances shifted; a woman married into one noble house might find her family on the opposing side in a conflict.

12.2 The Black Death (14th Century)

The Black Death, peaking in Europe around 1347–1351, caused widespread mortality. This event shook social structures and religious certainties. People faced the fragility of life daily, and some sources suggest a shift in how they viewed love and relationships. While it is hard to draw direct lines, the trauma of massive death likely influenced the emotional depth of personal bonds—some turned to more intense devotion, while others sought pleasure in a world that seemed unpredictable.

12.3 Shifts toward the Early Renaissance

By the late 14th and 15th centuries, the early Renaissance was stirring in parts of Italy. Scholars began revisiting classical texts, including works on love by Plato or Ovid. Courtly traditions, Christian ideals, and classical influences merged, setting the stage for a new chapter in Europe's cultural history. This does not mean medieval ideas about love vanished; rather, they blended with fresh approaches, eventually giving rise to Renaissance concepts of romantic devotion, artistic expression, and even changes in marriage customs.

CHAPTER 11

COURTLY LOVE IN THE HIGH

By the High Middle Ages—roughly the 11th to 13th centuries—Europe experienced significant social, cultural, and economic changes. Feudal structures matured, the Catholic Church grew in power, and trade routes expanded. In many noble courts, a new form of refined romantic expression arose, often called **courtly love**. While marriage in medieval society remained tied to property and alliance, courtly love represented an alternative sphere where passionate devotion, admiration, and personal longing were idealized—sometimes independently of marriage. This chapter explores the nature of courtly love, its social setting, the literary works that shaped it, and the controversies it provoked.

1. HISTORICAL CONTEXT OF THE HIGH MIDDLE AGES

1.1 Feudal Kingdoms and Aristocratic Courts

During the High Middle Ages, European kingdoms such as France, England, and parts of the Holy Roman Empire were governed by feudal elites. Noble families controlled vast estates, and the king or emperor relied on these lords for military support. Meanwhile, urban centers slowly grew, but the court remained the heart of aristocratic life. Royal and ducal courts were not just political centers; they were also cultural hubs, where nobles, knights, and ladies gathered for feasts, ceremonies, and entertainment. This environment allowed for a more elaborate social life than in earlier centuries, including the development of new literary forms.

1.2 Influence of the Church and Chivalric Ethos

The Catholic Church played a major role in shaping moral and social values. At the same time, the knightly class followed an evolving code of **chivalry**, which prescribed bravery in battle, loyalty to one's lord, and courtesy toward women. This mixture of Christian morality and chivalric ideals set the stage for courtly love: a highly stylized form of admiration, often directed toward a noble lady who was typically of higher status or already married. The tension between courtly desire and Christian ethics became a hallmark of the literature produced in noble circles.

1.3 The Growth of Vernacular Literature

Latin remained the language of church liturgy and scholarly texts, but vernacular languages—like Old French, Provençal (Occitan), and Middle High German—became vehicles for popular stories and poems. Poets and storytellers, sometimes supported by patrons, composed works for entertainment in aristocratic households. These narratives included epic tales of heroes, as well as romantic stories that praised refined love. Many of the earliest examples of courtly love literature appeared in the Occitan dialect of Southern France, influencing other regions.

2. DEFINING COURTLY LOVE

2.1 Core Elements and Terminology

The phrase "courtly love" (in modern English) is a later scholarly term. Medieval authors used various expressions—**fin'amor** (refined love) in Occitan, or **amour courtois** in Old French (though this exact phrase is rare). While the definitions vary, certain features recur in the texts:

- **Noble Setting**: The lovers are almost always nobles, usually from a royal or ducal court.
- **Idealization**: The beloved lady is placed on a pedestal, admired for her moral and physical qualities.
- **Secret Longing**: Often, the love is secret or discreet, especially if the lady is married to another man.
- **Service and Devotion**: The male lover behaves like a vassal, pledging loyalty, performing deeds to prove worthiness.
- **Refinement and Self-Improvement**: The struggle of unfulfilled love supposedly elevates the lover's character.

Though we talk of "love," the nature of these relationships is frequently non-physical in the poetry—an emotional bond or flirtation rather than a consummated affair. Authors emphasized the ennobling effect of longing, holding that sincere devotion could inspire moral growth.

2.2 Courtly Love and Marriage

Marriage in the medieval aristocracy was usually about property and alliances, leaving little room for romantic choice. Courtly love poetry, by contrast, focused on personal feeling, not practical concerns. The lady in question was often unattainable—either because she was married to the lord of the castle or because of her high status. This tension between formal marriage and private affection lent drama to the literature. Many historians think courtly love gave nobles an outlet for emotional expression outside the constraints of arranged unions. In real life, some of these courtly flirtations could remain innocent, while others might develop into actual liaisons.

2.3 Contrasts with Earlier Traditions
Before the High Middle Ages, love poetry existed in different forms. Latin poets of the late Roman world wrote about love, and so did earlier vernacular poets in the Germanic tradition. But the idea of a knight pledging himself to a distant, virtuous lady, craving her acknowledgment and bettering himself in the process, was a new literary phenomenon. Scholars debate whether influences came from Arabic poetry in Al-Andalus, from Celtic legends, or from unique French developments. Regardless, what emerged in the 12th century was a distinct cultural movement with lasting effects on European romance narratives.

3. SOCIAL FUNCTIONS OF COURTLY LOVE

3.1 Reinforcing Aristocratic Values
Courtly love worked within the feudal structure. By comparing the lover to a vassal and the lady to a lord, it affirmed hierarchical relationships. The suitor humbled himself, promising loyalty and service, just as a vassal served his lord. Many knights and nobles found this idea appealing because it complemented their existing sense of duty within the feudal system. At the same time, placing a lady in the role of "lord" subverted typical gender hierarchies, at least in theory. However, this reversal usually remained within the safe confines of poetic convention.

3.2 Entertainment and Cultural Refinement
Medieval courts placed great emphasis on **courtesy**—good manners, polished speech, and tasteful behavior. Courtly love poetry became a fashionable pastime, performed during feasts or gatherings. Noblewomen, in particular, hosted salons or smaller circles where poems were recited and discussed. This environment led to a culture of **"love debates"**, where participants argued about questions like "Does love exist without jealousy?" or "Which is better: a short, intense affair or a long, steady devotion?" These debates refined social interaction and showcased wit.

3.3 Potential for Real Emotion

Though often stylized, these courtly interactions could involve genuine emotion. Historical anecdotes mention aristocrats who risked scandal for the sake of romantic attachments, using courtly rhetoric. Some families tried to prevent certain knights from frequent contact with a married lady if rumors surfaced. Thus, while courtly love was partly a literary game, it could also overlap with real-life passions, generating both admiration and criticism within aristocratic circles.

4. KEY AUTHORS AND TEXTS

4.1 Andreas Capellanus and *The Art of Courtly Love*

One significant source is **Andreas Capellanus** (late 12th century), who wrote *De amore* (*The Art of Courtly Love*). This text, probably intended for an aristocratic audience, includes rules and dialogues about how a man should woo a lady of higher rank, plus sample conversations. It outlines the "stages" of love, from attraction to passionate devotion, and sets forth a code of behavior (like "He who is not jealous cannot love"). Scholars debate whether Andreas meant his work as a serious treatise or a satire on the excesses of courtly flirtation. Either way, it shaped discussions of courtly love for centuries.

4.2 Chrétien de Troyes and Arthurian Romance

In Northern France, the poet **Chrétien de Troyes** wrote Arthurian romances—like *Lancelot, or the Knight of the Cart* and *Yvain, the Knight of the Lion*—that featured strong courtly love elements. In these stories, knights undergo perilous quests for the favor of noble ladies, with personal desire adding emotional tension to chivalric deeds. The famous love affair of **Lancelot and Queen Guinevere** exemplifies the tension between loyalty to King Arthur and the irresistible pull of love. Chrétien's works helped popularize the theme of a knight who is morally tested by his devotion to both a lord and a lady.

4.3 Marie de France and Poetic Lais

Marie de France, an accomplished poet of the late 12th century, composed short narrative poems (lais) in Anglo-Norman French. Her lais often revolve around love, loyalty, and supernatural elements. For instance, in "Lanval," a neglected knight receives affection and aid from a mysterious fairy lady, sworn to secrecy. When he breaks his promise, he risks losing her love. Though not always labeled "courtly love," Marie's lais share common themes: love as a transformative, sometimes dangerous force, often set within noble or magical contexts. She highlights the emotional complexities faced by both men and women.

5. GENDER ROLES AND THE IMAGE OF THE LADY

5.1 The Lady's Elevated Status
In courtly love literature, the lady is typically portrayed as distant, higher in status, and morally superior. The lover idolizes her, praising her virtues and beauty. This depiction differs from the usual medieval reality, where women had limited legal rights and were often married off for family advantage. Literary idealization gave women symbolic power, at least within the framework of the poem or romance. She could command the lover to prove his worth, thus reversing the usual power dynamic.

5.2 The Lady's Real-Life Constraints
Outside of poems, noblewomen still faced arranged marriages, childbearing duties, and family obligations. While a few gained political clout—like Eleanor of Aquitaine, who championed troubadours—most lived under patriarchal norms. The gap between the poetic image of a commanding lady and the constraints of actual medieval life was evident. Some historians suggest that these idealized portrayals reflect men's fantasies of an untouchable, perfect woman rather than real empowerment for women. Still, many aristocratic women used the courtly love tradition to shape social gatherings, sponsor poetry, and elevate their cultural status.

5.3 Critiques of Courtly Love's Treatment of Women
Not everyone in medieval society agreed that these stylized relationships benefited women. Some moralists argued that praising a married woman's beauty or longing for her was sinful. Others pointed out that the woman is objectified, existing mainly as a moral or aesthetic ideal to inspire the knight. Real concerns about her personal feelings or autonomy rarely appear in these narratives. Yet, the tradition persisted because it fit within the cultural appetite for romantic escapism and refined social games.

6. LITERARY CONVENTIONS AND TROPES

6.1 Secret Meetings and Obstacles
Courtly love stories often feature clandestine encounters, coded messages, or symbolic gestures—like a token exchanged in private. Obstacles are key: a jealous husband, social distance, or moral constraints. These barriers heighten the emotional stakes. Unlike a typical marriage-based plot, where wedding ends the story, courtly love emphasizes the ongoing tension of separation or partial fulfillment. The idea is that longing itself refines the lover's soul.

6.2 Suffering and Joy
A hallmark of courtly love literature is the mixture of suffering (due to distance or rejection) and bliss (caused by the lady's slightest favor). The lover may languish, fall ill with longing, or perform dangerous feats just to earn a smile or a word of acknowledgment. Poets in the tradition used religious or near-religious language to describe the lady's presence. The intensity of feeling was considered a sign of genuine love, worthy of praise despite its challenges.

6.3 Moral and Spiritual Overtones
Some authors compare the lover's devotion to a spiritual quest. Though not exactly Christian worship, the language of adoration mirrors devotional practice. This blending of romantic and quasi-spiritual language led critics to question whether courtly love was borderline heretical. Others saw it as a harmless parallel, with no intention of replacing Christian piety. Regardless, the emphasis on pure, controlled passion allowed the tradition to avoid appearing too scandalous, though it never fully escaped controversy.

7. REAL-WORLD IMPACT AND PRACTICE

7.1 Noble Households and Courtly Manners
Within aristocratic households, the codes of courtesy extended to how men and women interacted. Jousts, tournaments, and festivals often featured a "Queen of the Tournament," a noble lady who gave out favors like ribbons to knights. Knights competed in her honor, reflecting courtly love's emphasis on winning a lady's approval. Such events were partly theatrical, but they also shaped real social behavior. Younger knights learned to address ladies with respect and to maintain refined conduct—even if actual marriages remained political and practical.

7.2 Courtly Affairs and Scandals
There are recorded instances of nobles engaging in secret relationships. Chroniclers sometimes mention adulterous affairs behind the façade of courtly admiration. For instance, the romance between **Abelard and Heloise**—though not strictly a "courtly love" story—demonstrates how passionate connections could clash with social norms. Abelard, a famed scholar, and Heloise, his student, entered a passionate affair that ended in public scandal and personal tragedy. While their story was more intellectual and less knightly, it showed the potential dangers of real passion in a structured society.

7.3 Church Reactions
Some churchmen criticized the concept of praising a married woman as if she

were an idol. They argued that it fostered lust and could lead to adultery. Others, however, appreciated the emphasis on virtue and self-control within the poetry, seeing it as a way to channel youthful energies into respectful admiration rather than crude misconduct. Over time, the Church had to balance its moral stance against the popularity of courtly literature. Local clergy might denounce certain songs or romances, but aristocrats often defended them as harmless entertainment.

8. CRITIQUES AND PARODIES

8.1 Literary Satire
Not all medieval writers praised courtly love. Some penned satirical works mocking knights who sulked about unrequited passion or ladies who toyed with their admirers. These parodies exposed the artificiality of certain courtly behaviors. **Jean de Meun**, in the second part of *The Romance of the Rose*, criticized idealized love, depicting it as a façade for sensual desire and vanity. His blunt tone contrasted sharply with the more delicate style of earlier troubadours.

8.2 Social Commentary
Moralists or practical-minded nobles sometimes dismissed courtly love as a distraction from real duties—like governing estates, raising armies, or maintaining social order. They claimed that knights wasting time composing poetry or pining for unattainable ladies were neglecting the harsh realities of feudal life. These critics believed that while courtesy was good, too much romantic musing undermined discipline.

9. EVOLUTION AND SPREAD

9.1 Regional Variations
Although the earliest center of courtly love was Southern France, the concept traveled to Northern France, England, Germany, and Italy. Each region adapted it. In Germany, **Minnesang** blossomed, featuring knights singing praises to lofty ladies (we will cover Minnesingers in Chapter 12). In Italy, poets like **Guido Guinizzelli** and later **Dante Alighieri** drew on courtly ideals, merging them with new spiritual perspectives in the "Dolce Stil Novo." Even as the local languages differed, the core idea of a noble, idealized love remained.

9.2 Late Medieval Adaptations
By the 14th and 15th centuries, courtly love motifs appeared in a wide range of works: from the **Canterbury Tales** by Geoffrey Chaucer to the romantic

allegories of Christine de Pizan. Some authors, while influenced by courtly traditions, added humor or realism, showing that not all knights were gallant, nor all ladies gracious. The tradition thus continued to evolve, influencing Renaissance courtship ideals as well.

10. LEGACY AND IMPORTANCE

10.1 Setting the Stage for Modern Romantic Ideals
Courtly love left a deep cultural footprint. It popularized the idea that true love involves personal devotion, moral betterment, and sometimes hidden longing. Over the centuries, Western literature and society adopted and adapted these themes. Even modern concepts of romantic relationships, which stress personal feeling over family arrangement, owe something to the medieval notion of love as an individual's passionate choice.

10.2 Criticisms and Ongoing Debates
Historians and literary scholars continue to debate the degree to which courtly love was practiced versus simply written about. Some see it mostly as a poetic fiction, while others argue that it shaped real relationships among the elite. Feminist critiques highlight that the lady's pedestal might be confining rather than liberating. Yet many still appreciate the artistry of troubadour lyrics, the complexity of Arthurian romances, and the tradition's influence on Western storytelling.

10.3 Transition into Later Eras
As we move past the High Middle Ages, the courtly love tradition blended with emerging Renaissance humanism. Writers like Petrarch carried forward the idea of longing for an idealized woman, yet they also embraced new views on individuality and classical learning. The transformation of courtly love set the stage for the love poetry of Shakespeare and beyond. Nevertheless, the medieval foundation of chivalrous devotion, secret yearning, and refined manners remained integral to how Europeans imagined romance.

CHAPTER 12

TROUBADOURS, MINNESINGERS, AND POETIC LOVE

During the High Middle Ages, the phenomenon of courtly love spread across different regions of Europe, inspiring diverse poetic traditions. Among the most notable were the **troubadours** of Southern France and the **minnesingers** of the Germanic lands. These poets turned love into a central literary theme, weaving music, verse, and social commentary together. Their works influenced not only noble courts but also the broader cultural landscape, setting standards for how love, devotion, and personal expression could be conveyed through poetry and song. In this chapter, we will explore the rise of the troubadours, the parallel movement of the minnesingers, the common themes and forms of their verses, and the impact they had on European ideas of romance.

1. THE RISE OF THE TROUBADOURS IN SOUTHERN FRANCE

1.1 Occitan Language and Courtly Culture
Troubadours were composer-poets who wrote in **Occitan** (also called Provençal), the language of Southern France. The earliest known troubadours emerged in the late 11th century, and the tradition flourished during the 12th and 13th centuries. Occitan was spoken in regions like Aquitaine, Provence, and Toulouse—areas known for relatively sophisticated courts and a certain cultural independence from Northern France.

The courts in these lands valued **fin'amor** (refined love) as part of their identity. Noble patrons supported troubadours, rewarding them for performances that celebrated courtly ideals. This environment, already fertile for the concept of love as an ennobling force, allowed the troubadours to thrive and experiment with lyrical forms.

1.2 Themes in Troubadour Poetry
Troubadour songs typically focused on:

- **Admiration of a Distant Lady**: The poet describes her beauty, virtue, and the joy or pain her presence (or absence) brings.

- **Love as Elevation**: The poet claims that by loving this noble lady, he improves himself morally and socially.

- **Suffering and Yearning**: Unfulfilled desire is a recurring motif, with the poet lamenting coldness or distance.

- **Secret Devotion**: Discretion and secrecy add intrigue, hinting that the lady may be married or otherwise unreachable.

Many troubadours used a **canso**, a standard song form, though they also invented other forms with strict rhyme and metrical patterns. Their verses were often sung or performed with instrumental accompaniment. While the subject was love, the poems could also contain subtle political commentary or personal rivalry.

1.3 Famous Early Troubadours

- **William IX of Aquitaine (Guilhem IX)**: Often cited as one of the first troubadours, he was a powerful duke who wrote lively, sometimes bawdy verses. His dual role as a politician and poet showcased how personal expression coexisted with feudal leadership.
- **Jaufre Rudel**: Famous for the theme of "love from afar," Rudel wrote about a distant lady he supposedly never met. Legend says he fell in love with the Countess of Tripoli purely from stories about her.
- **Bernart de Ventadorn**: A key figure who refined the love lyric, Bernart wrote many songs praising a lady's eyes, voice, and demeanor, while also expressing the anguish of rejection.

These troubadours established the tone for the next generations, blending praise, longing, and the courtly ideal of love's transformative power.

2. MINNESINGERS IN GERMANIC LANDS

2.1 The Emergence of Minnesang

In the German-speaking regions of the Holy Roman Empire, poets known as **minnesingers** (from "Minne," meaning love) began composing their own courtly songs in the 12th and 13th centuries. While influenced by the troubadours' emphasis on refined love, the minnesingers shaped a distinctive German tradition. Their language was Middle High German, and they performed in courts across regions like Swabia, Bavaria, and Austria.

2.2 Themes and Style

Minnesang shared many features with troubadour poetry:

- **Unattainable Love**: The singer praises a high-status lady, stressing his humble devotion.
- **Feudal Imagery**: The poet positions himself as a servant or vassal in love, seeking favor or recognition.
- **Moral and Spiritual Nuances**: Some minnesinger texts introduced elements of religious devotion, comparing the beloved's purity to a saintly figure.
- **Seasonal Imagery**: Many songs use references to spring or summer, connecting the renewal of nature to the awakening of love.

Minnesingers composed in forms like the **Bar form** (AAB), with complex rhythmic structures. Their performances often took place during festivals, court gatherings, or knightly tournaments. Over time, a subgenre called **Tagelied** ("dawn song") developed, depicting lovers parting at dawn to avoid being discovered.

2.3 Notable Minnesingers

- **Heinrich von Veldeke**: Considered an early link between French romance and German literature, he wrote both epics and love lyrics, helping to transplant courtly ideals into German-speaking courts.
- **Walther von der Vogelweide**: One of the most renowned minnesingers, Walther wrote on love, social critique, and political affairs. His love poems ranged from passionate devotion to more reflective musings.
- **Neidhart von Reuental**: Known for introducing peasant characters and rustic settings in his songs, creating a shift from purely courtly themes to a semi-comic look at love's tensions across social classes.

Minnesang thus offered variety: from high praise of noblewomen to playful or even satirical takes on romance.

3. POETIC FORMS AND PERFORMANCE

3.1 Musical Accompaniment and Courtly Events

Both troubadours and minnesingers typically performed their verses set to melodies. Stringed instruments like the lute, vielle, or harp might accompany them. In some courts, professional musicians performed the poet's works, while in others, the poet himself (or herself, in rare cases) sang. Audiences included aristocrats who prized lyrical skill. Love songs were the highlight of feasts, tournaments, or private gatherings in a noble hall.

3.2 Competition and Recognition

Troubadours and minnesingers often competed for patronage. Noble courts would host **tensos** (poetic debates) or contests where poets challenged each other on themes of love or artistry. Winners gained fame, gifts, or long-term support from a duke or count. This competitive spirit spurred innovation in rhyme schemes and melodic structure. Poets had to impress not only the patron but also the connoisseurs in the court, who were well-versed in the traditions of courtly love.

3.3 The Changing Status of Poets

In earlier medieval centuries, many poets were clerics writing in Latin. With the rise of troubadours and minnesingers, the poet's social role expanded: now he could be a nobleman, a knight, or even a lower-status individual supported by aristocratic patrons. The poet as a performer, traveling from court to court, became a familiar figure. This mobility helped spread poetic forms and love concepts across linguistic and regional boundaries.

4. COMMON THEMES IN TROUBADOUR AND MINNESINGER POETRY

4.1 The Distant Beloved

A recurring motif is the beloved who is physically or emotionally distant—maybe in another land or simply aloof. The poet's yearning intensifies because the lady's unattainability is linked to her social rank or her existing marriage. In the case of Jaufre Rudel, for example, his songs about loving the Countess of Tripoli from afar turned distance itself into a romantic subject.

4.2 Courtly Servitude

The poet portrays himself as a loyal servant to the lady. In minnesang, terms like *Dienst* (service) highlight this feudal metaphor: the singer pledges obedience as if she were his liege lord. Through this rhetorical stance, the poet shows humility and seeks moral elevation by loving someone 'above' him.

4.3 Joy and Despair
Troubadour and minnesinger lyrics oscillate between **joy** (when the lady offers a kind word or sign of favor) and **despair** (if she remains silent or critical). Poets call these moods **"joyful torment,"** reflecting the paradox that love's pains also signify its value. The poet's emotional states become a central drama, capturing an inner psychological world often absent in earlier medieval literature.

4.4 Morality and Spiritual Overtones
Some love lyrics subtly tie romantic longing to spiritual or ethical refinement. This synergy may reflect the era's religious mindset or a strategy to defend love poetry against accusations of frivolity. Poets claimed that love taught virtues like loyalty, humility, and kindness—mirroring Christian ideals. However, religious authorities sometimes disapproved of equating love for a mortal woman with a near-worshipful devotion, leading to ongoing tensions.

5. WOMEN POETS AND TROBARITZ

5.1 Existence of Female Troubadours
While medieval society restricted many women's public roles, a handful of female troubadours, known as **trobairitz**, composed Occitan poetry. Some are known by name, such as **La Comtessa de Dia** (Countess of Dia), who wrote moving songs from a woman's viewpoint. Her verses reflect the same courtly tradition but flip the perspective: here, the woman desires a beloved man and expresses frustration with his indifference.

5.2 Significance of the Female Voice
These trobairitz poems are rare but important. They show that women could also use courtly forms to articulate their longing or dissatisfaction. In society, most aristocratic women could not roam from court to court singing, as men did. But those with high status or personal determination might still find ways to share their verses. Their existence suggests that the phenomenon of courtly love was not exclusively a male creation—though it remained largely male-dominated.

6. POLITICAL AND SOCIAL INFLUENCES

6.1 The Albigensian Crusade and Decline in the South
In Southern France, the **Albigensian Crusade** (early 13th century) targeted heretical movements like the Cathars, resulting in widespread devastation. This

conflict undermined the local courts that had supported troubadours. Some troubadours fled to Spain or Northern Italy, reducing the artistic vitality of Occitan culture. Although the tradition survived for a while longer, it lost the robust patronage system it once had, leading to a gradual decline.

6.2 Courtly Circles in Germany
Meanwhile, German princes and dukes continued to support minnesingers. The **Hohenstaufen** emperors, like Frederick II, embraced court culture and intellectual pursuits. Minnesang flourished under their patronage, evolving stylistically over decades. Political shifts, however, also affected German lands, and by the 14th century, the minnesinger tradition began transitioning into newer forms of poetry, paving the way for **Meistersingers** in later centuries.

6.3 Cross-Cultural Exchanges
Troubadours and minnesingers traveled to various courts, sometimes crossing linguistic barriers. Northern French trouvères picked up Occitan themes, and certain minnesingers displayed influences from French forms. Merchants and aristocrats who moved between Europe's regions carried songs and ideas with them. This network of courts allowed for a continental culture of courtly poetry, even if each region adapted it differently.

7. LOVE DEBATES AND POETIC CONTESTS

7.1 Tensos and Partimens
Among troubadours, **tensos** (or **partimens**) were debate poems where two poets argued about love-related questions. One might advocate secrecy; the other, boldness. Or one might ask whether a man can truly love two women at once. These dialogues, often performed publicly, delighted audiences who enjoyed the wit and rhetorical skill. They also showcased the era's fascination with dissecting every angle of love and desire.

7.2 The Sängerkrieg (Minstrel Contest) Tradition
A famous example in German tradition is the **Sängerkrieg** ("minstrel contest"), a legendary contest said to have taken place at the Wartburg Castle. Minnesingers like Walther von der Vogelweide supposedly competed with skillful verses. Though partly myth, such stories reveal how crucial these contests were for building reputations. They also indicate that love was not just a private affair but a topic of public, performative engagement in front of nobles and courtiers.

8. EVOLUTION OF FORMS AND SUBJECTS

8.1 Later Troubadours
By the 13th century, some troubadours began writing more political or moral content. For instance, they commented on the Albigensian Crusade or local feuds. While love remained a central theme, the tone sometimes shifted. A few poets used the courtly style to criticize lords who broke feudal vows or to lament social injustice. This broadening of subject matter indicates how flexible the troubadour tradition was, even as it remained rooted in the language of refined emotion.

8.2 Expansion of Minnesang
In Germany, the minnesingers similarly diversified their topics. Some wrote poetry praising the Virgin Mary or referencing Crusade campaigns. Others used humor or parody to mock the seriousness of courtly devotion. By weaving in elements of daily life, moral lessons, or politics, they kept their art relevant to changing times. The core motif—love as a noble quest—still anchored the genre, but it could be adapted to reflect contemporary concerns.

9. CRITICISMS AND PARODIES

9.1 Tension with Religious Authorities
As with all forms of courtly love, the emphasis on earthly passion drew occasional criticism from the Church. Some clergy disapproved of songs that seemed overly sensual or that encouraged romantic longing for a married lady. Yet others appreciated the discipline, courtesy, and poetic skill, seeing them as lesser evils compared to crude behavior. Many courts found ways to reconcile these concerns by highlighting the moral dimension of respectful love.

9.2 The Mocking Genre
In both Occitan and German traditions, comedic or satirical poems poked fun at the high-blown language of love. Poets might portray a bumbling suitor or an unworthy knight who tries to imitate refined manners but fails. These works helped keep the tradition from becoming too rigid, revealing a self-awareness that not all love songs were to be taken at face value.

10. LEGACIES AND TRANSMISSION

10.1 Influence on European Literature
The troubadours and minnesingers were crucial in solidifying the concept of a poet-singer championing love in a vernacular language. Their forms and themes

influenced later traditions, like the **trouvères** in Northern France, the **Cantigas de amor** in medieval Spain, and the Italian **dolce stil novo** movement. Writers such as Dante Alighieri and Petrarch, often called the fathers of the Italian Renaissance lyric, inherited the courtly emphasis on admiration and the transformation of the lover's soul through devotion.

10.2 Manuscripts and Songbooks
Much of the troubadour and minnesinger repertoire was recorded in **chansonniers** (songbooks) or manuscripts compiled by scribes for wealthy patrons. Illustrations often accompanied the poems, showing knights in reverent poses before their ladies. These manuscripts became prized possessions. Although many were lost over time, surviving examples allow scholars to study the original Occitan or Middle High German texts, decipher musical notation, and understand the artistry involved.

10.3 Transition to Renaissance and Beyond
As the Middle Ages gave way to the Renaissance, some aspects of chivalric love persisted in new forms. The idea of the poet as a lover seeking to refine his soul influenced Renaissance humanists, who read medieval lyrics alongside classical works. Courtly traditions eventually merged with new modes of expression, leading to fresh developments in lyric poetry and the love sonnet cycle (e.g., Petrarch's sonnets to Laura).

11. ENDURING APPEAL AND MODERN INTERPRETATIONS

11.1 Romanticized View of the Middle Ages
In later centuries, people looked back at the troubadours and minnesingers as symbols of a romantic, idealized medieval world. The notion of a traveling poet with a lute, singing heartfelt devotion to a lady, captured the imagination of Romantic-era writers and musicians in the 19th century. This sometimes led to a simplified or sanitized image, glossing over the complexities and social constraints of the original context.

11.2 Scholarly Debates
Academics continue to debate the exact origins of the troubadour style, with theories pointing to Arabic poetry or Celtic legends. There is also ongoing discussion about how many of these love songs reflected real-life affairs versus purely literary conventions. The role of women, the sincerity of devotion, and the interplay of politics are all studied to understand the true nature of these poems.

11.3 Musical Revivals

Modern ensembles specializing in early music perform troubadour and minnesinger pieces. Although many melodies survive only in partial notation or uncertain form, musicians attempt reconstructions. Festivals in parts of France or Germany celebrate these medieval traditions, sometimes staging reenactments of poetic contests. The interest in historically informed performance shows that the mystique of courtly love and poetic singing still resonates.

CHAPTER 13

LOVE IN THE RENAISSANCE

The Renaissance, spanning roughly the 14th to the 17th centuries, was a period of significant transition in Europe. It emerged first in Italy—particularly in cities like Florence, Venice, and Rome—before influencing regions such as France, England, the Low Countries, and beyond. The word "Renaissance" means "rebirth," capturing the renewed interest in classical learning from ancient Greece and Rome. Alongside major developments in art, literature, and science, people also explored new ideas about human relationships, individual identity, and the nature of love. In this chapter, we will examine how love in the Renaissance took shape, influenced by classical ideals, religious traditions, and the changing social structures of the era. We will look at how courtship, marriage, poetry, and even the visual arts reflected this rebirth of knowledge and how it affected the way people expressed and understood romantic devotion.

1. SHIFTING FROM THE MEDIEVAL WORLD TO THE RENAISSANCE

1.1 Historical Context

By the 14th century, many parts of Europe were recovering from social and demographic upheavals. The Black Death (mid-14th century) had drastically reduced populations, affecting labor structures and changing economic relationships. Feudalism, so central in the Middle Ages, was slowly giving way in some regions to new forms of governance, urbanization, and a growing merchant class. Italian city-states like Florence, Milan, and Venice thrived on trade, banking, and commerce, producing wealthy patrons who could sponsor artists, scholars, and literary figures.

During the late medieval period, ideas of courtly love had been celebrated by troubadours and in chivalric romances. However, with the onset of the Renaissance, a humanistic perspective began to emphasize individual experience, critical thinking, and a return to the literary and philosophical texts of antiquity. This environment inevitably shaped how people approached love. No longer was love only framed by feudal obligations and the spiritual lens of the Catholic Church—though these influences did not vanish. Rather, intellectual curiosity about human nature led scholars and poets to explore love in more personal, philosophical, and sometimes secular ways.

1.2 Humanism and Its Influence on Love

Humanism, a defining movement of the Renaissance, placed the human individual at the center of intellectual inquiry. While devout Christian belief persisted, humanists wanted to reconcile classical philosophy (particularly that of Plato, Aristotle, and the Roman rhetoricians) with Christian doctrine. They emphasized the dignity and potential of man. This shift did not necessarily undermine religious faith, but it did encourage people to think more deeply about human emotions, including romantic love, from a personal standpoint as well as a spiritual one.

In contrast to much of the medieval focus on feudal or courtly ties, Renaissance humanists wrote treatises on civic virtue, ethical behavior, and the refinement of personal character. Love, under this lens, could be seen as a positive force that encouraged people to cultivate virtue, beauty, and harmony in their relationships. At the same time, the classical models offered new vocabulary to talk about love. The concept of "Platonic love," derived from Plato's works, became popular in certain circles, particularly in late 15th-century Florentine intellectual gatherings, adding new layers to how people described emotional bonds.

2. THE IMPACT OF CLASSICAL REVIVAL ON ROMANTIC IDEALS

2.1 Rediscovering Plato and the Idea of Spiritualized Love

One of the most striking literary developments of the Renaissance was the rediscovery of Plato's dialogues. While medieval scholastics had known Aristotle through Latin translations, Plato's works, especially on love, were reintroduced through Greek texts brought to Italy, often by Byzantine scholars fleeing the fall of Constantinople (1453). Among these texts, the *Symposium* and *Phaedrus* contained discussions about different forms of love—some more physical, some more spiritual.

Renaissance scholars like Marsilio Ficino (1433–1499), associated with the Medici-sponsored Florentine Academy, translated and commented on Plato's works. Ficino and others coined or promoted the concept of **Platonic love**, which suggested that attraction to physical beauty could lead the lover toward a higher, more transcendent appreciation of spiritual and intellectual beauty. This did not entirely reject bodily desires, but it proposed that true love should elevate the soul rather than fix it on mere earthly passion. Many Renaissance thinkers embraced this ideal, weaving it into discussions of courtship and human affection.

2.2 Literary Examples of Classical Influence

Poets and writers began to incorporate classical motifs and references to ancient gods of love—such as Cupid, Venus, or Eros—into their works. They blended these ancient symbols with medieval heritage. For example, one could find a poem praising a lady's features, but the poet would invoke Roman deities or Plato's concept of divine love to show how admiration of her beauty led to higher understanding or virtue.

Even within marriage treatises—some penned by humanist scholars—there was an effort to reconcile the classical notion of a virtuous, companionate marriage with Christian theology. While the Church still saw marriage as a sacrament primarily for procreation and social order, Renaissance writers increasingly highlighted companionship, friendship, and mutual respect as core aspects. This shift offered couples a new rationale for forging emotional bonds.

3. POETRY AND THE CELEBRATION OF LOVE

3.1 Petrarch and the Rise of the Love Sonnet

Francesco Petrarca (1304–1374), commonly known as Petrarch, is often credited with initiating a new lyric tradition that influenced European love poetry for centuries. Although he lived on the cusp between medieval and Renaissance culture, his work is emblematic of early Renaissance ideals. His sonnet sequence, known collectively as the **Canzoniere**, focused on his love for a woman named Laura. Though little is known about her historically, Laura became a literary muse for Petrarch's intense emotional outpourings, blending spiritual longing with earthly admiration.

Petrarch's sonnets refined the art of describing the beloved's physical beauty—eyes, hair, complexion—while also capturing the poet's inner turmoil of longing, guilt, and hope. The structure of the sonnet (14 lines, typically divided into an octave and a sestet in the Italian form) gave a concise framework for exploring the paradoxes of love. This form, which skillfully balanced personal emotion and rhetorical elegance, spread widely throughout Europe, inspiring poets in multiple languages.

3.2 Spread of the Sonnet Tradition

After Petrarch, the sonnet tradition took root in various courts. Italian successors like **Pietro Bembo** or **Baldassare Castiglione** wrote poems or treatises praising refined love. In France, poets of the Pléiade group, such as **Joachim du Bellay** and **Pierre de Ronsard**, adapted the sonnet style to French tastes. Their verses extolled ladies' virtues and lamented unrequited passions, continuing the Petrarchan tradition of the pained but devoted lover.

Meanwhile, in England, Sir Thomas Wyatt and Henry Howard, Earl of Surrey, introduced Petrarchan sonnets into English in the early 16th century. Later in the Elizabethan era, Shakespeare and others would create their own variations. Although this shift moves slightly beyond the strict boundaries of the Italian Renaissance, it illustrates how the concept of refined, introspective love poetry that started in Italy found resonance across Europe. Through these sonnets, love became both a personal confession and a literary art form.

3.3 Literary Salons and the Cult of the Muse

In many Italian city-states, aristocratic families and scholarly circles hosted gatherings where poetry was recited, music was performed, and debates on art and philosophy flourished. Women from influential families sometimes served as patrons or participants in these salons, encouraging poets to celebrate love in ways that reflected the new humanistic learning. The concept of a **muse**—a woman who inspired poetic or artistic creation—continued medieval traditions of the distant, idealized lady but was infused with Renaissance appreciation for classical forms and rhetorical eloquence.

Poets like **Gaspara Stampa** (1523–1554) and **Vittoria Colonna** (1492–1547) were notable female voices who wrote about love, devotion, and loss. They demonstrated that Renaissance love literature was not solely a male pursuit. Women, too, could turn to the written word to express personal feelings, though social constraints still existed.

4. COURTSHIP, MARRIAGE, AND SOCIAL STRUCTURES

4.1 Continuity and Change in Marriage Practices

Despite the flourishing of romantic ideals in poetry, Renaissance marriage among the nobility often remained a contractual alliance, arranged by families to secure wealth, power, or social prestige. Dowries continued to be significant in Italian cities, sometimes causing intense competition among families to offer large sums or valuable property so that their daughters could marry well. **Marriages were public events**, marked by elaborate feasts, processions, and sometimes civic celebrations, reflecting the union's importance for the wider community.

Yet, within this traditional framework, new ideas about companionship and mutual respect in marriage began circulating, influenced by humanist treatises. Authors like **Erasmus of Rotterdam** (1466–1536) argued that marriage should foster spiritual and intellectual friendship. Although his works were widely read, actual social practices changed more slowly. Commoners might have had more freedom to choose spouses based on affection, but they were also bound by family and economic considerations, especially in agricultural or craft-based households.

4.2 Women's Roles and Courtship Rituals

Patriarchy remained strong, meaning fathers or male guardians typically directed the marriage choices of daughters. However, in certain circles—particularly merchant or noble families that valued education—women gained a bit more literacy and exposure to humanist ideas. Some wrote letters, diaries, or poems, indicating they did reflect on personal emotions. Still, they rarely had complete autonomy in matters of love and marriage.

Courtship could sometimes be formal: if a family was favorable to a match, a suitor would pay calls to demonstrate respect. Love tokens such as rings, handkerchiefs, or miniatures might be exchanged. In Italian city-states, the presence of **carnival festivals** or public celebrations gave youth a chance to mingle, though strict social rules about modesty and public appearance persisted. For the wealthy, masked balls or musical gatherings could provide a setting for discreet flirtation under the watchful eyes of family chaperones.

4.3 The Concept of the Courtesan

In some Renaissance cities, particularly in Italy, the figure of the **courtesan** emerged—a woman who was educated, cultured, and served as a companion or entertainer for elite men. Though courtesans were often associated with sexual availability, many rose to prominence by virtue of their wit, artistic talents, and social skill. They might host salons, discuss literature, or compose poetry themselves.

This phenomenon reveals a dual attitude toward love and sexuality during the Renaissance. On one hand, there was admiration for cultured companionship; on the other hand, many courtesans were marginalized, their relationships existing outside the framework of marriage and Christian norms. Some became quite famous, patronized by princes or wealthy merchants, thus illustrating how the Renaissance city could foster both new forms of social freedom and entrenched inequalities.

5. PAINTING, SCULPTURE, AND THE VISUAL CULTURE OF LOVE

5.1 Renaissance Art and Love Themes

The Renaissance witnessed incredible achievements in painting, sculpture, and architecture. Artists like **Sandro Botticelli**, **Leonardo da Vinci**, **Raphael**, and **Michelangelo** gained renown for their skill in depicting the human form. Alongside religious subjects, classical myths and allegories of love appeared more frequently in art commissions.

For instance, Botticelli's works, such as **"Primavera"** and **"The Birth of Venus,"** depict mythological scenes celebrating beauty, fertility, and a gentle vision of love connected to classical ideals. The graceful figures, delicate gestures, and floral symbolism highlight a worldview where love is not merely physical but also a sign of harmony and virtue. Such paintings, often commissioned by wealthy Florentines, could serve as wedding gifts or decorations in palaces, reminding viewers of the refined and quasi-mythical dimension of love.

5.2 Portraiture and Matrimonial Symbolism

Portraiture gained new importance as families sought to commemorate dynastic ties. Wedding portraits might show a husband and wife, sometimes with subtle references to love or fidelity—a small dog symbolizing loyalty, flowers alluding to fertility, or inscriptions with a motto praising eternal devotion. These visual codes underscored the desired qualities in marriage: unity, fruitfulness, and prestige.

In Northern Europe, the Renaissance took its own form, influenced by the region's artistic traditions. Painters such as **Jan van Eyck** included minute symbolic details in portraits that indicated the emotional bond of a couple or the hope for a blessed union. The famous **"Arnolfini Portrait"** (1434) is often discussed for its portrayal of a merchant couple, possibly referencing themes of conjugal love and mutual trust, though its exact interpretation remains debated.

5.3 Sacred and Profane Love

A popular motif in Renaissance art was the distinction between "Sacred Love" and "Profane Love." In some allegorical works, a figure of Venus might appear twice—once modestly clothed, embodying sacred or spiritual love, and once nude, representing earthly or sensual love. The viewer was invited to reflect on how love could operate on different levels. This mirrored the philosophical debates influenced by Platonic notions of ascending from physical attraction to higher, divine-like affection. Wealthy patrons, fascinated by classical imagery, commissioned such works to display their erudition and taste, as well as to engage in subtle moral or intellectual commentary on the nature of desire.

6. COURT LIFE, PAGEANTRY, AND THE THEATER OF LOVE

6.1 Grand Festivities and Masques

Throughout Renaissance courts, extravagant festivals, tournaments, and masques were staged to honor visiting dignitaries, mark a noble wedding, or celebrate a significant civic event. These public spectacles often included allegorical tableaux about love, uniting classical mythology with the ideal of courtly refinement. Knights, sometimes dressed in classical costumes, jousted under banners referencing Cupid or the hearts of noble ladies. Meanwhile, specially composed music and poetry would extol the virtues of the bride and groom or praise the host's generosity and sense of culture.

Such pageantry echoed medieval chivalric traditions but with a Renaissance twist: references to ancient gods and the new learning replaced or combined with older feudal symbols. The theme of love as an ennobling challenge carried on, but its expression was more theatrical, shaped by the blending of Christian traditions, classical motifs, and the rising taste for elaborate set designs and costumes.

6.2 Dramatic Works and Comedies of Love

In Italy, the genre of **Commedia Erudita** developed—scholarly comedies in vernacular language often based on Roman playwrights like Plautus and Terence. These plays typically featured plots of romantic entanglements, mistaken identities, and generational conflicts, reflecting a lighter take on love and marriage. Though comedic, they sometimes revealed real social tensions, such as parental authority over marriage choices or the cunning strategies of young lovers seeking happiness.

Further north, in England, the late 16th century saw William Shakespeare produce plays that explored love in layered ways (though this edges into the Elizabethan era). Italian sources strongly influenced many of his comedies and romances, illustrating how Renaissance conceptions of love—at once classical, Christian, and courtly—could provide rich material for theatrical storytelling. Audiences were drawn to stories where love overcame societal barriers or comedic twists, suggesting that romantic devotion had an enduring appeal even in a changing world.

7. CONFLICTING VIEWS: LUST, SIN, AND THE PERFECT AFFECTION

7.1 Church Teachings on Love and Lust

The Renaissance did not dissolve the Church's moral authority. In Catholic doctrine, lust remained a sin if it divorced sexuality from the sacred bond of marriage. Confession manuals, sermons, and moral treatises continued to warn believers against adulterous or excessive passions. However, with the infiltration of humanist ideas, some theologians began differentiating between pure love that leads spouses closer to God and self-indulgent lust that degrades the individual.

Much of the Church's official stance still held that marriage was primarily for procreation and mutual support, but the humanist spirit introduced a more positive outlook on marital companionship. The concept of conjugal love as a kind of virtuous friendship grew in popularity, though it coexisted with older warnings against carnality. This tension is visible in the writings of Catholic moralists who found themselves praising the beauty of marital love while cautioning about lustful temptations.

7.2 Brothels, Adultery, and Social Realities

In many Renaissance cities, prostitution was regulated by local authorities. Official brothels existed in places like Venice, indicating a pragmatic acceptance of human desire outside the ideals of marriage. This acceptance did not mean moral approval—rather, city governments often argued that regulated brothels prevented worse social evils. Adultery, officially condemned, still occurred among nobility and commoners alike. In some cases, men and women who engaged in extramarital affairs used the language of courtly or Renaissance love to justify or glamorize their relationship, though if discovered, they might face severe social or legal penalties.

These contradictions highlight that while Renaissance love could be idealized in poetry and art, everyday life involved negotiation between moral codes, social pressures, and personal desires. Love could inspire moral improvement or lead to scandal and heartbreak. Authors of the time did not shy away from depicting such complexities, whether in satirical poems, comedic plays, or cautionary tales.

8. LATE RENAISSANCE DEVELOPMENTS

8.1 Changes in Political Structures and Their Impact on Love

By the late 16th century, nation-states like France, Spain, and England grew more centralized under strong monarchies. Diplomatic marriages between royal families became ever more critical for forging alliances. Love in these high-profile marriages often took a secondary place to political strategy. Yet, the Renaissance tradition of focusing on individual emotional experience continued to percolate. Royal courts, particularly in France under Francis I or in England under Elizabeth I, supported lavish cultural events celebrating love, loyalty, and noble virtues.

8.2 The Ongoing Influence of Petrarchism

Petrarchism refers to the style of love poetry that directly imitated Petrarch's language, imagery, and motifs. By the late Renaissance, this style had spread throughout Europe, leading to thousands of sonnets that repeated themes of the lover's sighs, the beloved's radiant eyes, and the internal conflict between desire and virtue. Some critics mocked the repetitive nature of these poems, labeling them formulaic. Others found in them a continued vehicle for genuine emotion. The tension between sincerity and cliché was already recognized in the 16th century, yet the tradition remained a robust form of poetic expression for new generations, partly because it provided a tried-and-true structure to discuss the complexities of love.

8.3 Transition to Baroque Expressions

As the Renaissance merged into the Baroque era (17th century), love poetry and artistic depictions took on new dramatic styles. Grand gestures, intense contrasts of light and shadow, and highly emotional music found in the early opera also affected how love was portrayed. Though we will explore the Baroque era in a later chapter, it is important to note that the Renaissance ideals of harmony, proportion, and classical reference set the foundation for these shifts. The story of love in Western culture would continue to evolve, but the Renaissance undeniably left its mark by emphasizing human individuality, emotional nuance, and the interplay between earthly desire and spiritual aspiration.

CHAPTER 14

LOVE AND THE REFORMATION

The 16th century was a time of religious upheaval in Western Europe. A movement initiated by Martin Luther in 1517, known as the **Protestant Reformation**, challenged the Catholic Church's doctrines and practices, leading to the rise of multiple Protestant denominations. Simultaneously, the Catholic Church embarked on its own reforms—often called the **Counter-Reformation**—in an effort to renew and defend its teachings. These seismic religious changes had wide-ranging social and cultural effects, including a profound impact on love, marriage, and family life. In this chapter, we will examine how the Reformation reshaped ideas about romantic relationships, the sanctity of marriage, the role of clergy, and the everyday practices that governed courtship and intimacy.

1. THE BACKDROP: RELIGIOUS AND SOCIAL TENSIONS

1.1 The Church Before the Reformation

Before the Reformation, the Catholic Church had held a near-monopoly on spiritual authority in Western Europe. Marriage was seen as one of the seven sacraments—an indissoluble bond overseen by the Church. Clergy were expected to remain celibate, and monasticism offered a way of life dedicated to spiritual pursuits apart from marriage. Many laypeople followed Church teachings on marriage and sexuality, though in practice, enforcement of moral codes varied widely from region to region.

However, by the early 16th century, widespread dissatisfaction arose concerning the sale of indulgences, clerical corruption, and the Church's powerful political role. Reform-minded thinkers questioned not only institutional abuses but also certain doctrines—among them, the nature of the sacraments and the authority of the pope. As discontent spread, it opened the door for radical changes in how believers conceptualized their relationship to God and to each other, including the relationship between husbands and wives.

1.2 Martin Luther and His Challenge

Martin Luther, a German monk and theologian, famously nailed his **Ninety-Five Theses** to the church door in Wittenberg in 1517 (according to tradition), criticizing the abuse of indulgences and calling for debate. This act, while initially focused on repentance and Church reform, unleashed a theological revolution. Luther argued that salvation came by faith alone, not through buying indulgences or following elaborate Church rituals. He also questioned the necessity of certain sacraments and the authority of the pope.

Luther, and later reformers like **Huldrych Zwingli** in Switzerland and **John Calvin** in Geneva, embraced the Bible as the primary source of religious truth. They rejected or modified many Catholic traditions. This doctrinal shift, known as **sola scriptura** (scripture alone), had a direct impact on how marriage was viewed. Protestant reformers taught that marriage was not a sacrament in the same sense as baptism or the Eucharist. Rather, it was an institution ordained by God for companionship, child-rearing, and moral well-being, but it did not confer grace in itself as Catholic sacramental theology suggested.

2. REFORMING MARRIAGE AND FAMILY

2.1 Ending Clerical Celibacy

One of the most revolutionary steps taken by Luther and other Protestant leaders was the rejection of mandatory clerical celibacy. Luther himself married a former nun, Katharina von Bora, in 1525, providing a high-profile example of clerical marriage. This action symbolized a broader theological position: that marriage was honorable for all Christians, including priests, and could serve as a setting for mutual support and godly living.

In Protestant regions, monastic institutions dissolved or were repurposed. Monks, nuns, and priests who converted to Protestantism often married, reflecting the new belief that marriage was not secondary to a supposed "higher calling" of celibacy, but rather a commendable and natural arrangement. This marked a dramatic cultural shift. However, not all segments of society agreed, and many Catholic regions maintained the traditional understanding of celibacy for clergy.

2.2 Redefining the Purpose of Marriage

Protestant reformers emphasized **three main purposes** of marriage:

1. **Procreation**: Bearing and raising children in a Christian household.
2. **Companionship**: Husband and wife providing mutual comfort and support.
3. **Protection Against Sin**: A legitimate outlet for sexual desire, preventing the temptations of fornication or adultery.

While medieval Catholic teachings also recognized these dimensions, the Protestant perspective de-emphasized the sacramental nature of marriage and instead highlighted it as part of God's creation order. Marriage was thus both a social institution and a personal covenant under God. This approach, in theory, elevated the emotional and relational aspect of marriage, making mutual love and respect more explicit reasons for uniting.

2.3 The Role of Women in the Protestant Household

In Protestant theology, the husband was still considered head of the household, reflecting broader patriarchal norms. However, wives were viewed as vital partners in the spiritual and practical management of the home. Reformers often praised the dignity of a Christian wife who raised children in faith and supported her husband's calling. Some women found greater autonomy in regions where convents closed, and they were free to marry or remain single outside monastic life.

Nevertheless, the new emphasis on the household as a "little church" meant that women's roles remained largely tied to domestic and family responsibilities. Education for girls sometimes improved in Protestant areas, since reading the Bible was seen as beneficial for all believers. But social structures continued to limit women's public roles, even though the religious rationale for female chastity or seclusion had shifted somewhat. In short, Protestant wives might have had a somewhat enhanced religious status, but they still operated within a patriarchal framework that expected obedience to husbands and devotion to household tasks.

3. LOVE AND MORAL REGULATIONS IN PROTESTANT COMMUNITIES

3.1 Emphasis on Moral Order

With the Reformation, many Protestant regions introduced stricter laws on moral conduct. Community leaders aimed to ensure that members of the newly reformed church lived according to biblical standards. This included regulation of sexual behavior, condemnation of adultery, and a closer scrutiny of courtship and marriage. In Calvin's Geneva, for example, the Consistory—a church court—investigated complaints of immorality, including improper relationships or marital discord. Punishments could be severe for those found guilty of breaches of the moral code.

Where medieval law had placed these matters largely under the jurisdiction of local bishops or canon law courts, the Reformation gave rise to new church structures that blended civic and ecclesiastical oversight. Magistrates and pastors collaborated to maintain community discipline, believing that a morally upright society was necessary to uphold true Christian faith. Marital love, in this view, was essential to spiritual well-being, and any disruption—a spouse's infidelity, for instance—threatened both personal salvation and the social order.

3.2 Weddings and Public Ceremonies

In Protestant communities, marriage rituals changed to reflect theological differences. While Catholic weddings remained sacramental, Protestant services often emphasized the couple's vows before God and the congregation, without framing it as a sacrament. The presence of a pastor and witnesses was still considered vital for legitimacy, but the liturgy was typically simpler, focusing on scripture readings and exhortations about marital duties.

Some regions established civil marriage requirements to ensure legal recognition of unions. Over time, the distinction between the sacred and civil aspects of marriage developed, with some Protestant areas leaning more heavily on state oversight. This shift set the stage for future debates about the extent to which marriage is a religious or civil contract—discussions that continue in various forms to this day.

4. CONTINUITY AND DIFFERENCES IN CATHOLIC REGIONS

4.1 The Catholic Counter-Reformation

The Catholic Church responded to the Protestant Reformation with its own internal reforms. The Council of Trent (1545–1563) clarified Catholic doctrine and addressed many administrative abuses. Regarding marriage, the Council reaffirmed its sacramental status. It also mandated that marriages be performed in the presence of a priest and witnesses to combat clandestine unions—a point that had caused legal and moral confusion in previous centuries.

By insisting on these requirements, the Catholic Church sought to solidify the sacramental nature of marriage, ensuring couples publicly declared vows in a formal liturgical setting. This was partly an effort to distinguish Catholic marriage discipline from Protestant practices, which allowed broader local variation. Catholic teachings continued to view conjugal love as tied to sacramental grace, though it also permitted the idea of mutual support and companionship as important within marriage. Yet no new acceptance of clerical marriage emerged; celibacy for priests remained a hallmark of Catholic identity, a clear line dividing Catholic from Protestant practice.

4.2 Catholic Views on Love and Conjugal Affection

Despite the theological disagreements, Catholic reformers also placed renewed emphasis on the importance of love and unity in marriage. Pastoral writings encouraged husbands and wives to see each other as partners in faith, reflecting the union of Christ and the Church (a longstanding analogy from earlier Christian tradition). The late 16th and 17th centuries saw an increase in the publication of Catholic "marriage manuals," guiding couples in spiritual and practical aspects of family life. These manuals, like their Protestant counterparts, tried to balance the call for moral purity with the recognition that spouses could and should care deeply for each other.

Therefore, while the Reformation triggered major doctrinal splits, Catholic families also experienced some cultural shifts: more consistent church oversight of weddings, clearer standards for annulments, and an elevated discourse about affectionate and respectful marital relations. The difference was that Catholicism insisted on marriage as a divinely instituted sacrament, inseparable from the Church's authority.

5. IMPACT ON COURTSHIP AND SEXUALITY

5.1 Changing Attitudes Toward Betrothals

Before the Reformation, clandestine or informal betrothals could result in disputes over whether a couple was truly married. The Protestant rejection of marriage as a sacrament did not necessarily eliminate these problems, but many Protestant territories tried to set clearer guidelines to avoid confusion. Public announcements of intent to marry (the "banns") and the requirement of formal ceremonies aimed to ensure couples entered marriage knowingly and with community support.

In Catholic regions, the Council of Trent specifically required that marriages be conducted in the presence of a parish priest and two witnesses to be valid—thus stamping out the possibility of secret betrothals that might later be contested. This arrangement also reinforced the importance of the local church community in overseeing the moral integrity of marital unions.

5.2 Courtship Norms and Parental Control

Though theological stances changed, the social reality of parental oversight in marriage choices continued in most areas. Family alliances, dowries, and considerations of social rank or property remained critical factors in both Protestant and Catholic societies. Where Protestantism did offer a slight shift was in the idea of personal conscience. Some pastors advised that a son or daughter's genuine consent was necessary to bless a union, reflecting the principle of individual faith. However, parents typically still held great sway, and an outright romantic "freedom of choice" was rare.

For ordinary people—peasants, artisans, or townsfolk—courtship often involved local customs, dances, or festivals. The Reformation's moral strictness sometimes introduced new taboos around courting rituals, but community life continued with certain amusements or gatherings where young people could meet. Church discipline targeted scandalous behavior, but healthy courting within recognized boundaries was usually tolerated.

5.3 Sexual Morality and Enforcement

Under Protestant regimes, offenses like fornication, adultery, and even "bundling" (where engaged couples slept in the same bed, sometimes separated by a board) came under stricter scrutiny. Church elders or consistories might penalize individuals found guilty of sexual sin, imposing public repentance or other punishments. Catholic areas also retained strong moral oversight, with Church courts or local rulers punishing extramarital affairs.

The intensity of enforcement varied: some Swiss cities, for instance, developed reputations for severe moral discipline, whereas in certain Lutheran regions of Germany, local attitudes might be more lenient. Yet overall, the Reformation era saw an effort to align personal romantic conduct with one's profession of faith. Love was good and godly if channeled within marriage; otherwise, it was suspect or sinful.

6. FAMOUS REFORMERS AND THEIR MARRIAGES

6.1 Martin Luther and Katharina von Bora

As noted, Martin Luther's marriage to Katharina von Bora became emblematic of the new Protestant view of clerical marriage. Katie Luther, as she was often called, was a former Cistercian nun. Their partnership showed a blend of practical responsibilities (she managed the household, finances, and even a brewery) and affectionate companionship. Luther's letters reference the warmth he felt for his wife, a striking change from the medieval assumption that a priest or monk should avoid marriage altogether.

6.2 John Calvin and Idelette de Bure

John Calvin, leading the Reformed tradition in Geneva, also married. His wife, **Idelette de Bure**, was a widow from an Anabaptist background who converted to Calvin's views. Their marriage was relatively brief (she died after about nine years), but surviving letters and references suggest a respectful, loving union. Calvin's theological writings stressed that marriage was a covenant under God, in which husband and wife shared spiritual, emotional, and social tasks.

6.3 Other Protestant Leaders

Many other Protestant pastors and reformers similarly took wives. This created a new social class of **clergy families**, setting examples for congregations on how a faithful Christian household should function. Pastors' wives often hosted gatherings, aided the poor, or taught younger women in the community, influencing the development of local religious culture. These real-life models helped normalize the idea that love and marriage were not only permissible for church leaders but also beneficial to church life.

7. CULTURAL EXPRESSIONS: LITERATURE AND ART

7.1 Protestant Hymns and Domestic Piety

As part of the Reformation's emphasis on congregational worship, leaders like Luther composed hymns or adapted folk tunes for religious use. Some of these songs touched on the theme of Christian fellowship that extended into family life and conjugal affection. The home was seen as a small church, where husband and wife taught children to fear God and love each other. Though not explicitly romantic in the sense of the earlier Renaissance sonnets, these hymns reflected a sense that daily life—marriage included—was sanctified by faith.

7.2 Literary Depictions of Love in Reformation Contexts

In Protestant regions, new literary genres emerged that combined moral lessons with entertaining plots. Elizabethan England (under Queen Elizabeth I, who was Protestant) saw the rise of drama exploring love, marriage, and conflict. Writers like Edmund Spenser, in **"The Faerie Queene,"** wove allegories about virtue and holiness into romantic chivalric stories, reflecting a complex interplay of medieval tradition, Renaissance humanism, and Reformation morality. Spenser's "Epithalamion," a poem written for his own wedding, celebrated marital union as both spiritually meaningful and personally joyful—a distinctly Reformation-age approach linking love to piety.

In Catholic regions, authors sometimes responded by reinforcing traditional ideals of sacral marriage, producing moral plays or treatises that held up the sacrament as a central pillar of community. A "holy couple" who participated in the sacraments and raised godly children stood in contrast, in Catholic eyes, to the perceived looseness of the new Protestant definitions, though from the Protestant perspective, Catholic marriages were burdened by superstition or excessive ritual. Literature thus became a battleground where each side extolled the virtues of its vision of love and marriage.

7.3 Visual Arts in Divided Christendom

Art, too, reflected these changes. In Protestant strongholds, the focus on biblical scenes, portraits, and moral narratives sometimes replaced the Catholic iconography of saints and sacramental themes. Painters from the Low Countries, like **Pieter Bruegel the Elder**, depicted peasant weddings with earthy realism, capturing communal feasting and dance. Although not overtly theological, such scenes resonated with Protestant ideas of everyday faith lived out in communal events, including marriage feasts.

In Catholic regions, the Counter-Reformation inspired lavish Baroque art celebrating the sacramental aspects of life, including marriage. Paintings might show the Holy Family as an ideal example of wedded love, or saintly couples who exemplified piety in their union. The Catholic emphasis on visible devotion and the grace imparted through sacraments found expression in dramatic, emotional imagery. The dividing lines in art were not always absolute, but the broader context of religious division informed how love, marriage, and family were visually portrayed.

8. LONG-TERM CONSEQUENCES FOR LOVE AND MARRIAGE

8.1 The Rise of Companionate Marriage

A notable long-term effect of the Reformation was the gradual growth of the idea of **companionate marriage**—a union based not solely on economic or dynastic concerns but also on emotional partnership, mutual respect, and shared faith. In both Protestant and reformed Catholic contexts, writers and preachers began to speak more frequently about the affective bond between spouses. Over time, this concept would gain momentum, paving the way for later Enlightenment and modern notions that emphasize personal choice and individual fulfillment in marital relationships.

8.2 Influence on Legal Structures

As Protestant states established national churches, civil authorities took a more direct role in regulating marriage. Over centuries, this helped lay the groundwork for **secular legal frameworks** around marriage and divorce. In some Protestant countries, divorce became legally permissible under certain conditions (like adultery or abandonment), challenging the absolute Catholic stance that a sacramental marriage was indissoluble except by annulment. This shift in the legal landscape signaled a reevaluation of marriage as both a spiritual and social contract.

8.3 Expanded Literacy and Vernacular Bibles

The Reformation, with its stress on reading the Bible in the vernacular, spurred literacy across many parts of Europe. More people could access scriptural teachings about love, marriage, and gender roles firsthand. Pamphlets, sermons, and household manuals circulated widely, offering advice on how a Christian couple should live. This proliferation of texts reinforced the idea that love, properly guided by God's word, formed the cornerstone of a stable household and, by extension, a stable society.

9. CRITICISMS AND TENSIONS

9.1 Conflicts Between Protestant Sects

Not all Protestants agreed on every point regarding marriage. The Anabaptists, for example, took more radical positions on community living and may have proposed different courtship norms. Meanwhile, Lutherans, Calvinists, and Anglicans each had their own rules about divorce, remarriage, and the exact nature of conjugal duties. These differences sometimes caused friction, as each group claimed to adhere more faithfully to Scripture.

9.2 Catholic-Protestant Hostilities

Religious warfare and persecution in the 16th and 17th centuries—such as the French Wars of Religion, the Thirty Years' War in the Holy Roman Empire, or England's shifting monarchs—shaped personal relationships across confessional lines. A Protestant man marrying a Catholic woman could become a lightning rod for suspicion or social ostracism. Love across religious divides was often discouraged, if not forbidden by local authorities. In some places, clandestine marriages did occur between members of different faiths, but such unions faced significant challenges.

9.3 Ongoing Patriarchal Constraints

Though reformers spoke of mutual affection, the fundamental patriarchal structure of marriage remained. The husband generally wielded authority; the wife was expected to be submissive. Women who deviated from the accepted norms risked censure. Even among radical sects that briefly entertained more egalitarian ideas, mainstream society reinforced women's subordination. Hence, while the Reformation era brought theological and legal changes, it did not necessarily grant women equal status in romantic or marital relationships.

CHAPTER 15

LOVE IN THE EARLY MODERN PERIOD

The Early Modern Period in Europe generally spans from the late 16th century through the 18th century. During this era, societies experienced large-scale transformations in politics, economics, science, and culture. Nation-states grew stronger, overseas colonies expanded, and social structures began to shift. These changes affected personal lives as well, including how people approached love, marriage, and family. In this chapter, we will look at how the developments of the Early Modern Period influenced romantic relationships, courtship practices, and the ways people expressed affection. We will also see the rising impact of commerce, literacy, and social mobility on ideas of love, as well as the continued role of religion in guiding moral standards.

1. HISTORICAL OVERVIEW: FROM REFORMATION TO STATE CONSOLIDATION

1.1 Political and Social Shifts

By the late 16th century, the Protestant Reformation had taken hold in various regions of Europe—Lutheranism in parts of Germany and Scandinavia, Calvinism in areas like Switzerland and the Netherlands, and Anglicanism in England—while Catholic territories, such as Spain, Italy, and parts of France, upheld the Counter-Reformation. These religious realignments continued to shape personal behavior and moral expectations. Yet, beyond religion, the rise of centralized monarchies and the growth of bureaucratic states also began to influence daily life.

Rulers like Louis XIV in France created large, centralized courts, employing ministers and officials to govern expanding territories. This period saw increased taxation, standing armies, and more direct state intervention in social affairs. Diplomatic marriages among the nobility remained a tool to form alliances, but governments also took a keen interest in population matters, including marriage laws and the moral conduct of citizens. This environment set a backdrop for how ordinary people experienced love and family life.

1.2 Economic Growth and Changing Social Classes

The 17th and 18th centuries witnessed expansions in trade, colonial ventures, and the beginnings of more global economic systems. New wealth poured into European ports, and mercantile classes—ship owners, traders, and merchants—rose in status. In cities like Amsterdam, London, and Hamburg, the merchant elite gained significant power. This shift gradually eroded some of the old feudal structures where noble families strictly controlled marriage alliances. While aristocrats still arranged unions to preserve dynastic interests, the growing middle classes also began to influence how marriages were contracted, focusing on property, commercial links, and sometimes personal preference.

Additionally, the early modern growth of towns encouraged social mobility. Apprentices, tradesmen, and artisans might prosper, earning enough income to improve their family prospects. At the same time, rural life remained bound by tradition, with peasant families often relying on local customs to guide courtship. People in both urban and rural environments tried to balance older community norms with emerging opportunities for individual choice and emotional closeness in relationships.

2. CONTINUITY AND CHANGE IN MARRIAGE PRACTICES

2.1 Arranged Marriages Versus Personal Choice

Despite centuries of evolution, arranged marriages did not suddenly vanish in the early modern period. For many noble and well-to-do families, marriage was still an alliance designed to protect land, titles, or commercial assets. Parents or guardians negotiated terms that included dowries, inheritance, and strategic connections. Yet, as the middle classes grew, certain families allowed sons and daughters more say in whom they married. Personal affection could tip the scales if the match was otherwise seen as suitable in social and economic terms.

Among the growing merchant class, matches were often made with an eye on business links. A daughter's dowry might help fund a new trading venture, and a son's marriage might bring in a partner's capital or trade connections. Within this setting, couples might also find room for personal attraction. Diaries and letters from the era show some wives praising their husbands' kindness or intelligence, revealing that love and respect could develop even within arranged frameworks.

2.2 Marriage Age and Changing Demographics

In early modern Europe, the average age of marriage varied by region and social status. In northwestern Europe (England, the Dutch Republic, parts of northern France), people tended to marry later—often in their mid- to late twenties—for economic reasons. They waited until they had saved money, secured a trade, or inherited a farm. This "Northwest European Marriage Pattern" contrasted with some Mediterranean or Eastern European regions, where people might marry earlier.

Later marriages meant many young adults spent years as servants, apprentices, or wage laborers before setting up their own households. This led to extended periods of courtship or single life, creating social contexts for flirting, festivals, or "bundling" customs (especially in rural areas) where couples might spend time together with partial privacy. Although the Church (Protestant or Catholic) often supervised moral behavior, communities still had local traditions that gave young people controlled opportunities to socialize.

2.3 Moral Standards and Religious Oversight

Throughout the early modern era, religious institutions—Protestant consistories in some places, Catholic parish priests in others—continued to monitor sexual conduct. Adultery, premarital sex, and illegitimate births could lead to church discipline or social stigma. In Protestant regions like parts of Switzerland or Scotland, community elders enforced strict rules, interrogating couples suspected of improper relations. Meanwhile, in Catholic countries, the Church's emphasis on confession and penance meant moral lapses might be addressed by local priests and, in severe cases, by ecclesiastical courts.

Yet, there was some variation in enforcement. Large cities sometimes tolerated discreet affairs among the wealthy, especially in more cosmopolitan centers like Paris or Venice, as long as they did not cause major scandal. Many authorities recognized the need for caution in punishing the powerful or those who contributed significantly to the local economy. This tension between moral ideals and practical governance shaped how strictly love and sexuality were policed.

3. COURTSHIP RITUALS AND EXPRESSIONS OF AFFECTION

3.1 Public Festivals and Community Traditions

In rural and small-town communities, local festivals, fairs, or seasonal celebrations provided structured times for youth to meet potential partners. Dances, singing competitions, or processions allowed mingling, though older community members kept watch. Young men might show off physical skills or small acts of gift-giving to impress young women, while young women might wear special ribbons or dress in fine clothing to indicate interest. These events often occurred under religious or civic auspices—harvest festivals, saints' days, or guild celebrations—blending communal identity with personal courtship.

In some regions, custom allowed a young man to visit a young woman's home under the supervision of family. These supervised visits (sometimes called "courting visits") aimed to maintain propriety while giving the couple time to converse. Certain traditions, like the aforementioned "bundling" in parts of Northern Europe or North America, involved the couple spending the night together partially clothed, presumably separated by a board or wrapped in blankets to maintain modesty. While frowned upon by strict moralists, these customs persisted in various forms, reflecting community norms that offered partial privacy but guarded virtue.

3.2 Love Letters, Poems, and Tokens

With rising literacy and the increased availability of paper, letter-writing became an important avenue for expressing affection in the early modern era. Couples who were geographically separated or subject to family supervision might exchange secret letters. These letters sometimes included coded phrases, references to shared experiences, or even lines of poetry. Historians studying such correspondence find evidence of real emotional intensity, along with careful negotiation of social barriers.

Poetry continued to be popular, though the styles evolved after the Renaissance. In many regions, "Petrarchan" styles of love poetry still thrived, but authors also blended local traditions or comedic elements. Chapbooks and printed pamphlets containing ballads of love or heartbreak circulated among broader audiences. The spread of printing technology allowed not just the elite but also moderately literate artisans or merchants to read romantic verses or moral stories about love. This enabled a wider cultural conversation about courtship and fidelity, sometimes featuring cautionary tales of seduction or betrayal.

3.3 The Role of Gifts and Small Gestures

Exchange of gifts—ribbons, gloves, rings, or embroidered handkerchiefs—remained a key way to signal affection. Such tokens often carried symbolic meanings: a ring for commitment, a handkerchief embroidered with hearts or initials for fondness, a pair of gloves representing protection or readiness to serve. In more affluent circles, jewelry might become a lavish demonstration of intent, while in simpler communities, handcrafted items held sentimental value.

These gestures did not always guarantee a formal engagement. Rather, they were part of a drawn-out process of showing interest, testing compatibility, and gaining community approval. If the relationship moved forward, families would meet to negotiate terms, set a date, and announce the match at church services.

4. LOVE IN THE UPPER CLASSES: COURT LIFE AND DIPLOMATIC MARRIAGES

4.1 Noble and Royal Households

In the courts of powerful monarchs, love and marriage continued to be entwined with politics and display. Young princesses and princes often found themselves betrothed to foreign nobles as part of alliances. Such marital agreements could help secure peace treaties or trade privileges. While personal affection was rarely the initial motivation, some of these couples forged genuine bonds over time, offering glimpses of real emotion within arranged frameworks.

Yet, among the nobility, extramarital liaisons were not uncommon. Kings or queens might keep favored courtiers as confidants or lovers, leading to intrigues and rivalries. At the French court, for instance, influential mistresses sometimes shaped political decisions. Moralists criticized these relationships, but courtiers often viewed them as part of courtly life. Some of these liaisons even adopted older patterns of "courtly love," with flattery, coded letters, and discreet rendezvous. Public scandal emerged only when jealousy or political rivalry spilled into open conflict.

4.2 The Emergence of Courtly Theater and Masques

Renaissance and Baroque courts loved theatrical displays, and the early modern era saw continued growth of lavish performances—masques, ballets, and plays—that revolved around love themes. During the reign of English kings James I and Charles I, for example, court masques written by playwrights like Ben

Jonson featured allegorical figures representing love, harmony, and virtue. Noble participants would dance and recite verses, creating a spectacle of refined culture. Such events projected the image of court as a place of elevated emotion and artistic brilliance, even if the daily politics of love were often more complicated.

In Italy, the tradition of **commedia dell'arte** brought a different flavor, with comic portrayals of love involving masked characters like Harlequin and Columbina. While these street or traveling troupe performances might not reflect the solemn court ideals, they entertained a wide range of audiences, sometimes poking fun at the pretensions of the elite. This type of theater occasionally touched on everyday love problems—jealousies, parental controls, or cunning servants assisting secret lovers—showing that the theme of love was not limited to solemn or high-brow forms.

5. THE RISE OF PERSONAL DIARIES AND INTIMATE WRITINGS

5.1 Greater Literacy and Private Reflection

As the printing press spread and literacy levels rose (especially in northern Europe), more individuals kept diaries or journals. These personal writings offer modern historians rare glimpses into the emotional lives of early modern people. Some diaries include confessions of love or guilt about romantic affairs, prayers for a spouse's health, or expressions of longing for a distant partner. Women, in particular, sometimes recorded their innermost thoughts about courtship or marriage, though surviving accounts remain limited compared to men's.

At the same time, letter collections from families reveal how siblings, cousins, or parents and children discussed prospective matches. Mothers might advise daughters on how to behave with suitors, or fathers might warn sons about untrustworthy ladies who only wanted money or status. This advice literature, both personal and published in pamphlets, underscored the idea that love was not purely a private emotion but a socially governed duty, shaped by moral and familial expectations.

5.2 Spiritual Autobiographies and Confessional Writings

In strongly Protestant contexts, believers sometimes wrote spiritual autobiographies, detailing their inner struggles with sin and redemption. Love for a spouse could appear in these texts as a reflection of God's grace, or as a potential distraction if it led to excessive worldly attachment. Meanwhile, in

Catholic regions, devout writers might reference personal devotions to the Virgin Mary or a favorite saint, weaving conjugal love into a broader tapestry of religious commitment. The personal journeys described in such writings show a world in which emotional life and spiritual beliefs were closely connected, with love operating at the intersection of personal desire and divine guidance.

6. WOMEN AND LOVE IN THE EARLY MODERN ERA

6.1 Female Education and Influence

While patriarchy remained the norm, the early modern period did see some progress in women's education among the upper and middle classes. In Protestant lands, reading the Bible in the vernacular was encouraged, meaning that daughters might learn to read at home. Certain Catholic regions also supported female education through convent schools, though these focused on piety and domestic skills. Educated women could compose letters, keep household accounts, and even write poems or spiritual reflections. Some aristocratic or bourgeois women thus gained a slightly greater voice in shaping their relationships.

In wealthy households, women might serve as cultural patrons, hosting literary gatherings or supporting artists. This sometimes extended to sponsoring romantic or moral plays, or even writing them. In rare cases, well-born women like the Duchess of Newcastle in England wrote treatises discussing love, marriage, and philosophy. These examples show that while most women remained under male authority, a small number managed to express their views on romantic life more publicly.

6.2 Constraints and New Possibilities

Despite these developments, the vast majority of women still had limited choices. Fathers or male guardians arranged marriages, and a woman faced social disapproval if she tried to reject a family-approved match. Divorce was either unavailable (in Catholic areas) or possible only under strict conditions (in Protestant states, typically for adultery or desertion). Widows sometimes gained a degree of autonomy, inheriting property or businesses, and thus could choose a second marriage partner more freely if they wished.

In some mercantile circles, wives worked alongside husbands in shops or craft businesses, sharing economic responsibilities and forging a partnership that sometimes led to deeper emotional respect. Still, women were expected to provide heirs, manage the household, and uphold moral standards. Love was deemed important but remained intertwined with duty and subordination. Social norms typically condemned extramarital relationships more harshly for women than for men, reflecting a double standard that persisted throughout the era.

7. LOVE ACROSS BORDERS: COLONIAL ENCOUNTERS AND GLOBAL EXCHANGES

7.1 Overseas Expansion and Marriage

The age of exploration and colonial expansion connected Europe with the Americas, parts of Africa, and Asia in new ways. Soldiers, traders, and colonists sometimes formed relationships with local populations. These unions varied: some were consensual, including intermarriage, while others involved coercion or abuse. In areas like Latin America, Spanish or Portuguese settlers might marry indigenous noblewomen to secure alliances. Meanwhile, in North America, English or French traders might form informal partnerships with indigenous women, bridging cultural divides for practical reasons like trade.

These relationships reflected both personal attraction and power imbalances. Documents mention "metis" or mixed families in places like New France (Canada), but such families had to navigate complex social prejudices. In some regions, colonial authorities tried to regulate marriage to maintain racial hierarchies or religious uniformity. Love could cross boundaries, but it often did so under unequal conditions shaped by conquest and economic motives.

7.2 Reports of Exotic Customs and Romantic Curiosity

Travelers and missionaries returning to Europe brought back accounts of different marriage rites and love practices. Some wrote about polygamy in certain parts of Africa or Asia, or the existence of divorce arrangements more flexible than European norms. These reports sometimes sparked curiosity or shock among European readers. They influenced philosophical debates—especially by the 18th century—about whether love and marriage were universal or culturally specific.

While these cross-cultural observations did not immediately transform European marriage law, they did contribute to a growing awareness that what Europeans considered natural or God-ordained might not be universal. Over time, such discussions would feed into Enlightenment-era questions about human nature, ethics, and the role of personal choice in marriage.

8. ARTISTIC AND LITERARY REFLECTIONS ON LOVE

8.1 Baroque and Classical Influences

In the 17th century, Baroque art and music often celebrated dramatic emotion, including love, but we will discuss the Baroque Era in detail in the next chapter. For now, it is important to note that early modern love stories in literature sometimes took a complex, psychologically richer approach than earlier medieval romances. Authors explored conflicting desires, moral struggles, and the tension between passion and social constraints. The Spanish writer **Miguel de Cervantes**, for example, used comic and reflective tones in works like *Don Quixote*, poking fun at chivalric ideals while also depicting heartfelt attachments among characters. Meanwhile, French playwrights like **Pierre Corneille** or **Molière** wrote dramas and comedies about honor, marriage, and the complexities of attraction within families aiming to preserve their status.

In England, William Shakespeare's later works and those of contemporaries like John Webster or Thomas Middleton tackled love through tragedies, dark comedies, and domestic dramas. Themes of jealousy, revenge, and desire highlight how love could lead to both personal growth and destructive impulses. These plays were popular across social classes, suggesting that the struggles and triumphs of love resonated widely. Audience members could see reflections of their own courtship or marital issues on stage, albeit in heightened form.

8.2 Popular Ballads and Chapbooks

Below the high literary culture, there was a vast array of popular ballads and chapbooks featuring tales of lovers parted by war, parental disapproval, or class differences. These short, inexpensive publications, often sold by traveling peddlers, gave rural and urban readers alike a chance to enjoy romantic stories. Sometimes they ended tragically—warning the young about the dangers of secret love or seduction—but others finished happily, affirming that genuine affection could conquer obstacles.

The popularity of such ballads reveals that, even in a world governed by arranged marriages and strict social codes, people yearned for narratives where love found fulfillment. This tension between romantic yearning and societal constraint forms a key thread in early modern popular culture, bridging the gap between lofty courtly dramas and everyday concerns.

9. NEW IDEAS EMERGING: TOWARD THE ENLIGHTENMENT

9.1 Growth of Intellectual Debates

As the 17th century progressed, scientific breakthroughs (by figures like Galileo, Descartes, and Newton) and philosophical shifts began to reshape European thought. While these changes did not directly overthrow traditional marriage patterns, they did encourage a spirit of inquiry and skepticism. Thinkers started asking questions about human nature, emotions, and social contracts. The budding Enlightenment interest in individual rights and reason hinted that personal choice in love might become more important in future discussions.

Debates about love and marriage cropped up in pamphlets or early philosophical works. Some writers questioned the moral strictness of certain church authorities or proposed that marriages based on mutual affection were more stable. Others stuck firmly to the view that paternal authority must guide a couple's union. This variety of opinions set the stage for broader intellectual confrontations in the 18th century, when Enlightenment figures would take these questions even further.

9.2 Seeds of Legal and Social Reform

In some regions, small reforms in marriage law appeared. For instance, certain Protestant states allowed for divorce in limited circumstances—an idea that would have been unthinkable in medieval Catholic Europe. Meanwhile, in Catholic lands, the Council of Trent's mandates made marital record-keeping stricter, which helped formalize the process. These shifts, though modest, gave states a clearer role in documenting and overseeing marriage. Over time, government officials, not just church leaders, would issue marriage licenses or register births.

This emerging legal framework hinted that marriage might eventually be seen as partly a civil contract, not merely a religious sacrament. The practice of public banns, enforced by both Catholic and Protestant authorities, tried to ensure that communities knew about intended unions, giving local folks a chance to voice objections. Such procedures aimed to protect the couple from fraudulent or bigamous arrangements but also placed individual love in the hands of the broader society.

CHAPTER 16

THE BAROQUE ERA AND LOVE

The Baroque era, stretching roughly from the early 17th century to the mid-18th century, was characterized by dramatic artistic styles, powerful absolute monarchies, and ongoing religious and political conflicts. This period witnessed an intensification of emotional expression in art, music, and literature—a theatrical quality that also shaped people's ideas about love and relationships. Building on the transformations of the Reformation and the Early Modern period, the Baroque world continued to blend older feudal or courtly traditions with emerging social structures. In this chapter, we will explore how love was expressed and experienced during the Baroque era, focusing on the rise of absolute courts, the role of the Catholic and Protestant churches, and the influential forms of art and music that gave new voice to romantic emotions.

1. HISTORICAL CONTEXT: ABSOLUTE MONARCHS AND CONTINUING RELIGIOUS TENSIONS

1.1 The Rise of Absolutism

By the 17th century, several European states consolidated power under monarchs who aspired to near-complete authority. The best-known example is Louis XIV of France (reigned 1643–1715), who famously declared, "L'État, c'est moi" ("I am the state"). Other rulers, like the Habsburg emperors in Austria and the princes of various German states, followed forms of centralized governance, though with varying degrees of success. These monarchs often sponsored extravagant courts, where nobles were required to attend and display loyalty. The culture of these courts significantly influenced love and marriage among the elite, weaving personal desires into political intrigue.

At the French court in Versailles, for example, Louis XIV shaped social norms by regulating etiquette, fashion, and how nobles interacted. Courtiers vied for royal favor, forming a swirl of gossip, alliances, and discreet (or sometimes open) affairs. While marriage among the high nobility remained largely a matter of political arrangement or property consolidation, personal attachments flourished beneath the surface. Such relationships sometimes led to scandal, but if handled with subtlety, they could become part of a noble's social strategy.

1.2 Aftermath of the Religious Wars

The 17th century was marred by conflict like the Thirty Years' War (1618–1648), which devastated large parts of the Holy Roman Empire. These religious and political upheavals shaped how communities viewed moral life and personal bonds. In Catholic regions, the Counter-Reformation continued to stress the sacramental nature of marriage, encouraging families to uphold strict moral norms. In Protestant regions, various forms of Calvinist, Lutheran, or Anglican discipline persisted. At times, local councils or consistories still investigated breaches of sexual morality, though enforcement could differ widely.

Despite these official stances, love maintained a complex role. Ordinary people carried on with courtships, marriages, and the pursuit of affection, navigating whichever religious or secular authority governed their area. The acceptance or condemnation of certain relationships often depended on whether they threatened social stability. While arranged marriage was the norm, especially among the wealthy, the emotional dimension of romantic attachment was beginning to gain more public expression in literature, music, and theater.

2. COURT LIFE, SPECTACLE, AND LOVE

2.1 Grandeur at Versailles and Other Courts

One hallmark of the Baroque was the spectacular nature of court life. Kings, princes, and high nobles hosted grand balls, masques, and elaborate ceremonies that dramatized social hierarchies. At Versailles, Louis XIV demanded constant attendance from nobles, effectively turning them into courtiers dependent on his favor. This close-quarters existence led to a climate where flirtation, hidden romances, and strategic displays of affection became part of daily survival. If a noble formed a romantic attachment, it had to be managed discreetly to avoid damaging alliances or offending the king.

Courtly love as an ideal did not vanish, but it adapted to the Baroque taste for ostentation. Courtiers performed gallantry, wrote flattering verses to ladies of rank, and participated in choreographed dances that symbolized their social roles. The elegance of the period's fashion—ornate dresses, flowing wigs, and sumptuous fabrics—contributed to a heightened awareness of physical presence and visual allure. Love at court, therefore, was often theatrical, with carefully chosen gestures meant to impress both the beloved and onlookers.

2.2 Royal Mistresses and Courtly Influence

Many absolute monarchs kept official or unofficial mistresses. In France, Louis XIV's liaison with Madame de Montespan and later Madame de Maintenon was an open secret. Elsewhere, Charles II of England famously had multiple mistresses who gained public attention. These relationships were not purely personal: the king's mistress often wielded real political influence, sometimes controlling appointments or shaping policy decisions. While moralists criticized such arrangements, the power dynamics of the court made them difficult to uproot.

For noblewomen, becoming a royal mistress could bring patronage, wealth, and social leverage—but also envy, rivalry, and moral censure. The complex interplay between official marriage, extramarital attachments, and personal passion formed a daily reality in Baroque courts, reflecting the tension between public duty and private desire. In some cases, the mistress was acknowledged in court ceremonies, further blurring lines between legitimate marriage and romantic attachments.

2.3 Baroque Festivities and Allegorical Love

Just as earlier periods featured masques and pageants, the Baroque took them to a new level of extravagance. Courtiers might organize mythological tableaux representing Venus and Mars, or Cupid and Psyche, symbolizing themes of love, beauty, and conquest. These spectacles combined music, dance, lavish costumes, and stage machinery—reflecting the era's fascination with drama. By adopting allegories of classical gods and heroes, participants framed their own romantic pursuits in a context of cosmic or mythic significance.

Such events reinforced the idea that love was both a personal sentiment and a public performance. Even weddings among the nobility were opportunities for theatrical display, sometimes with commissioned operas or ballets extolling the couple's union as harmonious and beneficial to the realm. This fusion of real matrimony and staged allegory was quintessentially Baroque, merging daily life with art in a grand spectacle.

3. BAROQUE RELIGIOSITY AND MARITAL IDEALS

3.1 Intensified Religious Sentiment

While the Reformation and Counter-Reformation had already reshaped religious life, the 17th century continued to see strong expressions of faith. In Catholic lands, a renewed emphasis on devotional practices and emotional piety flourished. Mystics like St. Teresa of Ávila (in the late 16th century) had set a precedent for intense personal devotion, and Baroque Catholicism expanded on this with dramatic sermons, lavish church art, and devout confraternities. In Protestant regions, certain revival movements encouraged heartfelt personal faith. Pietism in Germany, for example, placed importance on inward religious experience.

These devotions influenced how people thought about love and marriage. Sermons might compare the believer's relationship to God with the bond of a bride to a groom, urging spiritual fidelity. Couples were advised to see their union as part of a larger divine plan—particularly in Catholic communities where marriage remained a sacrament symbolizing Christ's bond with the Church. Meanwhile, in Protestant contexts, a pious household was praised as a "little church," with husband and wife sharing scriptural duties and moral responsibilities.

3.2 Moral Discipline and Clandestine Love

Religious authorities of all confessions often continued to police sexual behavior. However, enforcement could vary by region or decade. In some Catholic territories, local inquisitions or church courts monitored any conduct that deviated from orthodoxy, including secret affairs. In Puritan-influenced regions (like parts of England under Oliver Cromwell or certain American colonies), strict moral codes prevailed, punishing adultery or promiscuity harshly.

Yet, clandestine love did not disappear. Noble lovers used private chapels or remote estate wings to conduct affairs away from prying eyes. Town dwellers might frequent discrete meeting places if they dared defy moral norms. For many, love was a domain where human passion collided with religious law, resulting in a perpetual push-pull. Some individuals found legitimate avenues—like marriage based on affection—while others risked censure or ruin for unapproved attachments.

4. OPERA, MUSIC, AND THE THEATRICAL EXPRESSION OF LOVE

4.1 The Birth of Opera in Italy

One of the most influential Baroque inventions was opera, emerging in Italy around the turn of the 17th century. Early composers like Claudio Monteverdi in Mantua and Venice blended music, drama, and lavish stagecraft, often centering on stories of love—both tragic and triumphant. Opera's unique power lay in its ability to convey intense emotion through music, capturing the highs and lows of romantic passion.

Works like Monteverdi's "L'Orfeo" (1607) and later Francesco Cavalli operas set Greek myths of love and loss to music, enthralling aristocratic audiences. Opera houses became cultural hotspots where nobles, wealthy merchants, and foreign travelers came to experience the spectacle. Love on the Baroque operatic stage was heroic, grand, and frequently tragic—reflecting the era's fascination with emotional extremes.

4.2 Opera's Spread Across Europe

Opera quickly spread beyond Italy. In France, Jean-Baptiste Lully developed a distinctive style of French opera under Louis XIV's patronage, often incorporating balletic interludes that showcased the king's own dancing prowess in earlier decades. These works included romantic subplots, sometimes praising the glory of the monarch or the harmony of the realm. In England, Henry Purcell introduced semi-operas and masques featuring enchanting love songs—such as "Dido and Aeneas"—where the queen's lament over lost love became a poignant Baroque moment.

Opera's rise fed into the broader culture of courtly entertainment, reaffirming that love was an emotional force worthy of public celebration. Audiences wept at the suffering of parted lovers or rejoiced at their eventual unions. The art form mirrored the tension between public spectacle and private feeling, a cornerstone of Baroque emotional life.

4.3 Love Duets and Emotional Depth

Central to Baroque opera were love duets, in which two singers portrayed lovers, each voice intertwining in harmony. These duets encapsulated the era's ideal of love as a powerful, often turbulent union—a "conversation" of melodic lines that could express devotion, jealousy, longing, or despair. Composers used dissonance, ornamentation, and harmonic progression to heighten emotional impact, echoing the swirl of real-life romantic entanglements at the time.

Though these stage stories were fictional or mythic, they resonated with audiences who recognized parallels to their own experiences. The polished veneer of courtly manners contrasted with the raw emotion displayed in aria after aria, suggesting that behind the refined façade of Baroque society lay deep wells of passion. Opera thus bridged the gap between personal feeling and communal performance, turning love into a shared cultural drama.

5. BAROQUE VISUAL ARTS AND LOVE

5.1 Grand Paintings and Symbolic Imagery

Baroque painting, known for its dynamic compositions, strong contrasts of light and shadow (*chiaroscuro*), and intense emotional appeal, offered another medium for expressing and shaping ideas about love. Artists such as Peter Paul Rubens in Flanders or Gian Lorenzo Bernini (more famed as a sculptor in Rome) depicted mythological and religious scenes that often involved themes of desire, devotion, or divine union. Rubens, for instance, painted lush, fleshy figures brimming with vitality, occasionally illustrating the loves of gods and goddesses, or allegories of marriage uniting rival nations.

Religious art also took on a heightened sense of emotional fervor, with saints like Mary Magdalene or Teresa of Ávila shown in states of ecstatic devotion. While not romantic love in the secular sense, such depictions carried a language of passion and rapture that sometimes paralleled human longing. Baroque art blurred the lines between sacred and profane love, demonstrating the era's fascination with intense feeling, whether directed toward God or a human beloved.

5.2 Bernini's Sculptures of Ecstasy

Gian Lorenzo Bernini's sculptures, especially in Rome, displayed an unparalleled ability to capture movement and sensuality in stone. His famous work, "The Ecstasy of Saint Teresa," in the Cornaro Chapel, shows the mystic saint swooning in religious transport as an angel pierces her with a divine arrow—an image that merges spiritual union with a physical expression reminiscent of romantic or erotic ecstasy. This synergy of bodily rapture and holy love stirred controversy among some viewers who found it too sensual, yet it perfectly encapsulates the Baroque spirit of mingling divine ardor with human passion.

Other Bernini sculptures, such as "Apollo and Daphne," depict mythological love pursuits: Apollo chasing the nymph Daphne who transforms into a laurel tree to escape him. The swirling drapery and lifelike tension evoke the agony and thrill of unrequited love. Audiences in the 17th century admired these works for their technical brilliance and their emotional immediacy, reflecting an era where love—even love that ended tragically—could be the subject of awe and wonder.

5.3 Patronage and Marital Portraiture

As in earlier epochs, wealthy families commissioned portraits to commemorate marriages or alliances. During the Baroque era, these portrait sessions could become theatrical. Artists like Diego Velázquez in Spain captured royal couples in grand attire, placing them within splendid palace interiors. The emotional bond between spouses might be subtly indicated by the closeness of their posture or a shared gaze—though the public message emphasized dynastic continuity.

Such portraits served as propaganda for ruling dynasties or noble houses, reassuring subjects that their leaders personified unity and strength. In smaller-scale noble or merchant portraits, couples might be depicted with symbols of fidelity (such as dogs) or references to their mutual prosperity (like well-tended gardens). Love here was not purely personal; it was also a statement of social stability and cultural refinement, consistent with the Baroque love of grandeur.

6. THE EVERYDAY EXPERIENCE OF LOVE: BEYOND THE COURT

6.1 Middle-Class and Artisan Households

While the courts dazzled with spectacle, most Europeans lived more modest lives. Artisans, merchants, and farmers typically followed communal patterns for courtship and marriage. In many Protestant regions, the church congregation took a keen interest in ensuring young couples followed moral guidelines. Banns were read to announce pending marriages, and neighbors might celebrate a wedding with local feasting and dancing. The emotional content of these marriages varied, but personal affection could develop within or alongside the family's economic considerations.

In Catholic communities, priests remained a guiding force. Confession, marriage instruction, and parish events shaped the moral framework for love. Couples were expected to approach marriage as a sacrament, preparing with prayer and penance. Despite the seriousness of religious obligations, local festivals or carnival seasons often allowed playful expressions of romantic interest. Young people might exchange small tokens, share a dance, or build personal connections—always aware of the watchful eyes of relatives and neighbors.

6.2 Literacy, Letters, and Self-Expression

As printing and literacy advanced, more ordinary citizens could read pamphlets, moral tracts, or even love ballads. This exposure to new ideas about romance might encourage some to see love as a more personal, heartfelt choice rather than a mere arrangement. Still, practical concerns like dowry, land inheritance, or trade partnership carried heavy weight. Diaries and letter collections from the period show a mix of pragmatic reasoning and genuine tenderness. A merchant might write home to his wife while traveling for business, expressing both worry over finances and longing for her companionship.

In rural areas, strong communal norms persisted. Gossip and local custom regulated conduct, ensuring that couples who flaunted social or religious rules might face censure. Elopements occasionally occurred when families disapproved, but such unions risked legal complications if not recognized by church or state authorities. Despite these challenges, couples sometimes found ways to marry for love, weaving their emotional ties into the tapestry of social expectations.

7. GENDER ROLES AND EMOTIONAL BONDS

7.1 Women's Position and Obedience

The Baroque era continued the patriarchal patterns of earlier times. Women, especially in noble or bourgeois families, were expected to obey fathers and husbands. Marriage treaties among the elite served dynastic or financial interests, with brides sometimes sent far from home to cement alliances. Emotional fulfillment for these women was unpredictable—they might form close bonds with their husbands, or they might find themselves in a loveless partnership. Some sought emotional satisfaction in motherhood, friendships with other ladies of the court, or discreet romantic attachments.

For the majority of women in working-class contexts, marriage was a partnership in running a household or a small business. Love could develop through daily cooperation, childrearing, and shared struggles. But legal rights were limited; divorce was rare or complicated in Catholic areas, and even in Protestant regions with some divorce provisions, women rarely initiated the process. Widowhood could grant a measure of independence, letting a woman manage finances or remarry by her own choice—yet that autonomy was hard-won and often tinged with social constraints.

7.2 Men's Emotional Responsibilities

Men, too, navigated a complex emotional landscape. Aristocratic men had to balance the duties of public life—military service, court attendance, or administrative roles—with family obligations. Some relished public displays of gallantry and flirtation. Others invested emotionally in their wives or devoted themselves to paternal roles. Common men—peasants, artisans, or small-scale merchants—spent long hours laboring for their families. Their expressions of love might be more practical: providing resources, building a sturdy home, or ensuring children's well-being.

In both high and low social spheres, cultural norms encouraged men to appear strong, rational, and not overly sentimental. Nonetheless, personal letters reveal that men did express affection, longing, and worry for their spouses or sweethearts—emotions sometimes concealed in public but revealed in private writings. The period's moral codes expected men to control their passions, especially lust, though extramarital affairs were tolerated for powerful men far more than for women, highlighting a persistent double standard.

8. INTELLECTUAL CURRENTS: EARLY SCIENCE, REASON, AND LOVE

8.1 Scientific Revolution's Indirect Influence

Figures like Galileo Galilei, René Descartes, and Isaac Newton introduced radical new ways of understanding the cosmos and the human capacity for reason.

While these developments did not explicitly redefine love, they fostered a growing emphasis on observation, rationality, and questioning traditional authority. This cultural environment gradually laid the groundwork for Enlightenment philosophers who would, in the 18th century, debate the nature of human emotions and social contracts more explicitly.

During the Baroque era itself, the notion that love might be explained or analyzed in more secular, human terms was slowly gaining ground among some intellectual circles. Certain treatises on moral philosophy or "civility" began to address the management of passions, including romantic desire. Writers observed that while love could be a source of virtue and happiness, it could also lead to irrational behavior. The tension between reason and passion remained a central theme, foreshadowing more extensive Enlightenment discussions.

8.2 The Philosophical Salon

In places like Paris, literary salons run by aristocratic or learned women gained popularity. These gatherings brought together nobles, writers, and thinkers to discuss art, philosophy, and manners. Love, as a topic, surfaced in debates over the proper comportment of men and women, the moral or immoral nature of passionate liaisons, and the possibility of love as a path to self-improvement. Salon hostesses—like the Marquise de Rambouillet or later the Marquise de Sévigné—curated conversations that often touched on romantic ideals, exploring how they intersected with refined manners and wit.

While these salons did not overturn social norms regarding marriage, they did highlight an interest in exploring love as more than a fixed arrangement. Conversation about courtship, gallantry, and the emotional interplay of the sexes introduced a slightly more nuanced view, laying cultural seeds that would grow into the Enlightenment's more critical stance on tradition. Even so, strong hierarchies and moral codes limited how far these discussions could challenge official or familial dictates.

9. COLLIDING FORCES: LOVE, WAR, AND SOCIAL STRIFE

9.1 Effects of Prolonged Warfare

The 17th century's major conflicts, such as the Thirty Years' War or smaller-scale wars between France and neighboring states, disrupted families and communities. Soldiers were often away from home for years, leaving wives to manage farms or households alone. Some couples maintained love through letters, though illiteracy or the chaos of war could hamper communication. War also led to displacement, famine, and disease, undermining the stability needed for courtship and marriage.

In some war-torn regions, young people delayed marriage, or families clung to tradition more fiercely. The need to rebuild after destruction sometimes created opportunities for different social classes to intermarry—if, for instance, entire villages were depopulated. Love stories set against the backdrop of war highlight the fragility of personal bonds when overshadowed by national or dynastic conflicts, a theme that would appear in Baroque literature and drama.

9.2 Social Unrest and Witch-Hunts

The Baroque era also saw episodes of social panic, such as the witch-hunts in various parts of Europe and North America (particularly in the late 16th and 17th centuries). Fear of demonic influence occasionally spilled over into accusations involving love charms, "poisoning husbands," or seducing men through sorcery. Women with knowledge of herbal remedies or midwifery were vulnerable to suspicion if neighbors envied or disliked them.

Though not directly about romantic love, these accusations show how the intense climate of fear could distort normal relationships. A scorned lover might claim witchcraft to explain heartbreak. Communities that enforced strict moral codes might demonize any behavior seen as subversive or promiscuous. Such incidents underscored the precarious position of those who stepped outside accepted norms in love and sexuality.

CHAPTER 17

THE ENLIGHTENMENT AND CHANGING VIEWS

Spanning much of the 18th century, the Enlightenment was an intellectual and cultural movement that championed reason, progress, and individual rights. Philosophers, scientists, and writers questioned traditional authorities—be they monarchs, churches, or ancient texts—and called for reforms in government, education, and society. This shift in worldview profoundly affected personal relationships, including ideas about love, marriage, and family. In this chapter, we will explore how Enlightenment thinkers challenged older norms, proposed new ideals for companionate marriage, debated women's roles, and set the stage for modern notions of romantic autonomy.

1. BACKDROP: THE 18TH-CENTURY WORLD IN FLUX

1.1 Intellectual Momentum from the Scientific Revolution

By the early 18th century, the achievements of the Scientific Revolution—exemplified by Newton's laws of motion, Cartesian rationalism, and new empirical methods—had convinced many European elites that human reason could unlock nature's secrets. Enlightenment figures extended that optimism to moral and social realms. If reason could govern the universe, perhaps it could also guide human behavior, relationships, and governance. This placed older structures—feudal obligations, absolute monarchies, rigid church doctrines—under scrutiny.

For love and marriage, this meant reevaluating whether religious tradition or aristocratic custom should dominate personal unions. Philosophers asked: Should couples not be free to choose spouses based on affection and compatibility? Can women be seen as rational partners rather than property transferred in a dowry contract? These questions did not instantly upend all social norms, but they introduced a potent new discourse about love grounded in reason, mutual respect, and the pursuit of happiness.

1.2 The Rise of Public Opinion and Print Culture

The 18th century saw an explosion in print culture: newspapers, journals, pamphlets, and books became more accessible, fueling a "public sphere" where ideas were debated. Coffeehouses and salons in cities like London, Paris, and Berlin served as hubs for discussion. People read novels, political tracts, and philosophical treatises, forming opinions that sometimes clashed with official or aristocratic viewpoints.

Among these publications, novels about love gained popularity, featuring heroines and heroes who navigated social constraints. Writers like Samuel Richardson in England or Jean-Jacques Rousseau in France explored the internal emotional lives of characters, stressing personal virtue and sincerity. Such stories resonated with a growing middle-class audience that valued individual feelings and moral sentiment. This literary culture both reflected and shaped the period's evolving views on love.

2. ENLIGHTENMENT PHILOSOPHERS ON LOVE AND MARRIAGE

2.1 John Locke and the Concept of Social Contract

Although John Locke (1632–1704) lived in the late 17th century, his works profoundly influenced the 18th century. Locke argued that governments derive their authority from a social contract with the governed, emphasizing individual rights to life, liberty, and property. While he did not write extensively on marriage as a parallel social contract, many of his followers reasoned that if political power depends on consent, perhaps marital relations should as well. This line of thought suggested that spouses might enter marriage for mutual benefit, rather than merely obeying tradition.

Locke's ideas about rational individuality also fueled debates on education. His Some Thoughts Concerning Education promoted nurturing reason in children—boys and girls, although he said less about girls. Over time, such educational reforms nudged parents to see children as individuals with personal inclinations, which indirectly affected how future marriages were arranged or permitted. The seeds of personal choice in courtship were being sown.

2.2 Montesquieu, Voltaire, and the Critique of Society

French Enlightenment thinkers like Montesquieu and Voltaire examined social and political structures, occasionally touching on marriage and family. Montesquieu's *The Persian Letters* (1721) used fictional Persian visitors in Europe to satirize French customs, including forced marriages or the seclusion of women. While comedic, it questioned whether love and happiness could flourish under rigid social constraints. Voltaire, known for his wit and anticlerical stance, criticized the hypocrisy of some church laws regarding marriage, though he did not systematically propose alternatives.

These thinkers saw love as part of broader social life—subject to the same critical scrutiny as religion or monarchy. While they did not all champion radical reforms for women or marriage, they contributed to a climate where questioning old norms was fashionable. Enlightenment salons frequently hosted debates on the virtues of companionate marriage, the tyranny of parents in match-making, or the potential for divorcing an unfaithful or abusive spouse. Though progress was slow, the intellectual conversation was changing.

2.3 Jean-Jacques Rousseau and Sentiment

Jean-Jacques Rousseau (1712–1778) played a pivotal role in Enlightenment thought on emotions and nature. In his novel "Julie, or the New Heloise" (1761), Rousseau presented a story of intense romantic feeling clashing with social obligations, illustrating the conflict between personal happiness and societal expectations. The book became a literary sensation, inspiring many readers to empathize with characters torn by love and duty. Rousseau argued that authentic sentiment and moral purity could counteract the corruptions of modern society.

In his treatise "Émile" (1762), Rousseau discussed education, suggesting that a well-raised individual would grow into a virtuous adult capable of genuine love. He proposed distinct roles for men and women—men active, women modest—but also insisted that the marital bond should rest on mutual respect. While some see Rousseau's views as reinforcing traditional gender roles, others note that his emphasis on sincerity and emotional authenticity paved the way for more open discussions about romantic love's importance.

3. EMERGENCE OF THE COMPANIONATE MARRIAGE IDEAL

3.1 Defining Companionate Marriage

An important Enlightenment development was the rise of companionate marriage—the notion that emotional closeness, shared moral values, and mutual affection should be central to marriage. While practical considerations like property and status remained significant, Enlightenment writers insisted that a marriage founded solely on economic or dynastic motives risked unhappiness and moral decline. A union of two rational beings, joined by love and respect, was held up as an ideal.

This did not overturn arranged marriages overnight, but it provided a philosophical justification for couples (especially in the middle class) to seek personal compatibility. Some families, influenced by Enlightenment ideas, began to allow children more say in choosing spouses, hoping that an affectionate match would result in a stable home. The idea of "falling in love" before marriage gradually gained acceptance, at least in certain circles, though it coexisted with older norms throughout the 18th century.

3.2 Middle-Class Adoption of the New Ideal

The burgeoning middle classes—merchants, professionals, manufacturers—proved receptive to these ideas. Their homes, no longer strictly subject to feudal obligations, could become showcases of domestic virtue and affection. Manuals on child-rearing and household management extolled the mother-father partnership, each playing a distinct but complementary role. Wives were encouraged to be companions to their husbands, offering intellectual and emotional support rather than simply managing servants.

Literature and periodicals geared toward middle-class readers, such as the Spectator in England or various French moral weeklies, depicted marriage as a potential source of personal fulfillment. They carried stories of modest couples who overcame social obstacles to wed for love, thereby exemplifying virtue and reaping rewards. The message: True love within marriage was not only possible but morally superior to the cynicism of purely arranged unions. Although patriarchal constraints remained, the emphasis on companionship in these publications signaled a slow cultural shift.

3.3 Critiques and Ongoing Realities

Not everyone embraced companionate ideals. Some aristocrats scorned them as bourgeois sentimentality. Others worried that if individuals chose mates based on inclination, social hierarchies might erode. Even among Enlightenment intellectuals, paternal authority and social rank weighed heavily. Many marriages still involved parental or communal approval, dowry negotiations, and strategic alliances. Emotional compatibility was an aspiration rather than a guaranteed outcome.

Moreover, women's legal rights were limited. A woman who married for love might still find herself legally bound to an unkind husband, with few recourses for escape unless she had wealth or influential relatives. Thus, while companionate marriage ideology advanced, it coexisted with structural impediments. In Catholic regions, divorce remained inaccessible, and even in Protestant lands that allowed it for certain causes, it was rarely granted. Enlightenment talk of emotional equality within marriage often collided with laws that designated wives as subordinate.

4. LITERATURE, THEATER, AND THE CULT OF SENSIBILITY

4.1 The Rise of the Sentimental Novel

By the mid-18th century, novels focusing on personal feeling—often called sentimental novels—proliferated. Writers like Samuel Richardson in England penned works such as "Pamela, or Virtue Rewarded" (1740), portraying a servant girl pursued by her master. Through tearful trials, Pamela's steadfast virtue and emotional sincerity eventually lead to a socially upward marriage. Such plots underscored the moral and emotional worthiness of love, even across class divides.

In France, Marivaux authored comedies and novels exploring delicate emotional interplay among lovers. His style, known as "marivaudage," captured subtle changes of heart and the complexities of flirtation. This literary fascination with the interiority of love—how hearts change, how misunderstandings arise—resonated with Enlightenment audiences intrigued by human psychology. Characters were praised for sincerity, softness, and empathy—qualities deemed essential for genuine affection.

4.2 Sensibility and Emotional Refinement

A wider cultural trend known as "sensibility" or "sentimentality" emphasized sympathetic feeling, compassion, and an acute awareness of moral and emotional nuances. People believed that refined souls naturally expressed empathy for others' suffering and delicacy in romantic matters. This ethos prompted men and women to cultivate tender sensibilities—crying over heartbreak in novels, cherishing sentimental tokens, and seeking deep connections with loved ones.

Critics of sensibility mocked it as excessive or hypocritical, citing instances where the outward display of emotion overshadowed consistent moral action.

Yet the movement undeniably expanded the conversation about love beyond mere duty. Romantics, heartbreakers, sympathetic onlookers—each found a place in a cultural narrative that prized emotional authenticity. The emphasis on feeling laid the groundwork for the Romantic Movement that would follow, though Enlightenment thinkers generally preferred balancing sentiment with reason rather than indulging unbridled passion.

4.3 The Stage: Comedies of Manners and Bourgeois Dramas

Theater continued to explore love themes in both comedic and serious forms. In France, Pierre de Marivaux and Voltaire contributed to comedic plays where misunderstandings in love tested the wit and virtue of characters. In England, Oliver Goldsmith and Richard Brinsley Sheridan wrote comedic "plays of manners," poking fun at the pretensions of high society while championing sincere love among the relatively virtuous.

Meanwhile, the "bourgeois drama" emerged in Germany, with playwrights like Gotthold Ephraim Lessing (in works like "Minna von Barnhelm," 1767) depicting middle-class protagonists who overcame obstacles to achieve a union based on mutual respect and genuine feeling. These plays and comedies offered moral lessons about the hazards of greed, deception, or class snobbery, implying that a love guided by honest sentiment was the key to social harmony. Audiences across Europe found these stories relatable, reflecting real tensions around marriage choices, parental authority, and personal desire.

5. WOMEN'S VOICES AND EARLY FEMINIST THOUGHT

5.1 Limits to Women's Independence

Despite the Enlightenment's celebration of reason, equality, and human rights (for men), women mostly remained confined to traditional roles. Laws rarely granted them independence, and the new ideals of companionate marriage often reinforced the notion that a woman's place was in the private sphere, supporting her husband. Many male philosophers—Rousseau included—argued that women's education should focus on making them better wives and mothers, not on cultivating intellectual autonomy.

Nevertheless, some women found opportunities to articulate their ideas. Certain salon hostesses and authors argued for women's capacity to reason and to love as equals. They pointed out contradictions in Enlightenment rhetoric that espoused liberty while keeping half the population subordinate. This tension marked an important stepping stone toward modern feminist thought, even if changes to the legal status of women remained minimal in the 18th century.

5.2 Notable Female Writers on Marriage and Love

In England, Mary Astell (1666–1731), an earlier figure, wrote "A *Serious Proposal to the Ladies*" (1694), urging women to seek education and self-improvement. She famously questioned the institution of marriage: "If all men are born free, how is it that all women are born slaves?" While Astell was devoutly religious, she nonetheless challenged the complacency of women who accepted subservience. Later, writers like Charlotte Lennox, Fanny Burney, and others wrote novels depicting heroines navigating love with wit and moral resolve, implying that women's feelings mattered as much as men's.

In France, female intellectuals like Madame de Staël (though she belonged partly to the following generation) drew from Enlightenment ideas to critique social constraints on women's freedom to choose loving partners. She and others recognized that the companionate marriage ideal could only flourish if women had a say in the union. A few bold voices demanded that marriage be reformed to allow women property rights or easier separation from abusive spouses, though these calls rarely led to legal changes in the 18th century.

6. MARRIAGE REFORMS AND LEGAL DEBATES

6.1 Inheritance and Property Concerns

Enlightenment debates about individual rights extended to property and inheritance. Some thinkers proposed that women should retain property after marriage or at least have stronger legal claims. However, entrenched systems of male primogeniture and paternal authority were not easily dismantled. In Catholic regions, church laws remained, requiring marriages to be solemnized in church, while in Protestant areas, secular authorities sometimes introduced subtle reforms.

For instance, in parts of northern Europe, local ordinances might loosen regulations on betrothals or clarify conditions for divorce. The impetus was not purely romantic sentiment; states wanted to reduce bigamy, quell disputes over legitimacy, and ensure that property transfers were transparent. Nonetheless, even small legal shifts had an impact on how families negotiated marriages. The principle that individuals had personal interests—financial and emotional—gained traction, though actual practice varied by class and locale.

6.2 The Continuing Struggle for Divorce Rights

Enlightenment discourse did not universally champion liberal divorce laws, but it did highlight contradictions. Philosophers asked: if a marriage is truly a contract, should it not be dissolvable when the contract is fundamentally broken? The Catholic Church still refused to permit divorce, allowing only annulments in rare cases. Protestant territories that allowed divorce did so under narrow conditions (adultery, desertion, impotence), making it an extreme measure seldom pursued.

A few Enlightenment figures—especially in more radical circles—argued that forced cohabitation without mutual affection was unnatural, but conservative forces prevailed. The notion that marriage might be ended because of incompatibility or personal unhappiness was too radical for the mainstream. Only in certain jurisdictions, like some German principalities, might judges grant divorces more frequently—but the stigma remained high, and women rarely had the financial or social leverage to claim them.

7. CROSS-CULTURAL ENCOUNTERS AND IDEAS OF NATURAL LOVE

7.1 Travel Literature and "Exotic" Customs

As colonial expansion continued, Enlightenment-era travelers and philosophers took keen interest in comparing European customs to those of indigenous peoples in the Americas, Africa, or Asia. Some Enlightenment writers praised certain "primitive" societies for their perceived simplicity in courtship and marriage, arguing that European practices had become corrupt or overly governed by property concerns. Others condemned polygamy or arranged marriages in foreign lands as backward, ironically ignoring Europe's own restrictive traditions.

Philosophical works referencing these travel accounts debated what was "natural" in love and marriage, sometimes concluding that personal choice and emotional bonds were closer to nature's intention than complex dowry negotiations. However, these discourses were often tainted by colonial prejudices and superficial understandings of other cultures. Still, the comparative perspective encouraged some to question the rigidities of European marriage law and to explore alternative views on romantic attachment.

7.2 The Myth of the Noble Savage and Innocent Love

Writers like Rousseau popularized the concept of the "noble savage," imagining that indigenous peoples, unspoiled by civilization, engaged in purer forms of emotion. While this idea was idealized and rarely accurate, it influenced Enlightenment thinking by positing that humans, in a "state of nature," might experience love more authentically. Some romantic narratives set in faraway lands used this trope, showing European protagonists learning deeper truths about love from "simpler" societies.

Despite the problematic stereotypes, these stories and philosophical musings contributed to a growing belief that love should be freed from excessive artifice and social constraint. The contradiction was that these same philosophers often maintained paternalistic or racist attitudes toward the very peoples they romanticized. Nonetheless, the motif of "natural love" remained in circulation, fueling 18th-century debates on whether Europe's structured marriages smothered genuine affection.

8. INFLUENCE ON DOMESTIC LIFE AND CHILD-REARING

8.1 The Home as a Site of Emotional Fulfillment

Enlightenment emphasis on reason and sentiment elevated the domestic sphere as a realm where personal relationships could flourish. Manuals on child-rearing and household management increasingly portrayed the home as a refuge from worldly corruption, a place to nurture virtue through affectionate parenting and spousal harmony. Women, cast as moral guardians, were praised for creating a loving environment, while men were urged to show kindness and restraint, not brute patriarchal authority.

This ideal significantly impacted how couples might conceive of their marriage. If the household was a microcosm of rational benevolence, then mutual respect and companionship were essential. This perspective underscored the shift from marriage as a purely external alliance to an inward-facing partnership, aiming for emotional satisfaction and moral edification. While the reality of daily life—financial stress, labor demands, or class disparity—often undermined these ideals, the Enlightenment vision of a warm, emotionally fulfilling home persisted.

8.2 Parental Affection and Fewer Wet Nurses

Previously, aristocratic or affluent families often sent infants to wet nurses or employed them in-house, limiting mother-child bonding. Enlightenment discussions about natural child-rearing, spurred partly by Rousseau's *Émile*, encouraged mothers to breastfeed their own babies and maintain closer physical contact. This approach suggested that love and tenderness, starting in infancy, formed the foundation of a virtuous adult life.

Such shifts in child-rearing, while not universal, indicated a broader cultural move toward recognizing emotional attachments within the family as beneficial and morally significant. Fathers, too, were urged to engage with children, guiding them through reason and gentle discipline rather than fear. In effect, the Enlightenment project extended the concept of loving relationships to the entire family structure, not just between spouses.

9. CRITICISMS, BACKLASH, AND THE LIMITS OF ENLIGHTENMENT REFORM

9.1 Accusations of Moral Degradation

Traditionalists in church and state often accused Enlightenment proponents of undermining social order. They worried that if love and individual choice were elevated, respect for authority—paternal, religious, or monarchical—would erode. Satirists depicted the new emphasis on sentiment as leading to frivolous affairs or disrespect for elders. In some regions, laws were tightened to prevent "runaway matches," ensuring parental control remained strong.

Moreover, the concept of "free love" was rarely advocated by mainstream Enlightenment figures, many of whom still believed in moral restraint and the importance of stable families. So the tension was not between a libertine revolution and a conservative establishment, but rather between those who wanted moderate reforms in line with reason and feeling, versus those who defended inherited structures vigorously.

9.2 Continuance of Social and Legal Constraints

For all the talk of reason and sentiment, 18th-century Europe largely maintained patriarchal norms. Women in many places lacked legal standing to own property independently after marriage. Royal and noble families continued to arrange marriages for dynastic reasons. The church—Catholic or Protestant—remained heavily involved in marriage rites and moral policing. The concept of love as a personal, emotional bond was thus aspirational. Enlightenment ideals did not immediately dismantle centuries of tradition.

Still, the seeds of transformation were planted. More families allowed some input from children on marital choices. Some Protestant states recognized broader divorce grounds, albeit narrowly. In intellectual circles, the idea that couples should be free to form attachments based on mutual respect gained currency. By the century's end, revolutionary movements—especially the French Revolution—would challenge existing power structures in ways that also affected laws on marriage and divorce. But that lay just beyond the scope of the typical Enlightenment period.

CHAPTER 18

THE ROMANTIC MOVEMENT AND LOVE

By the late 18th and early 19th centuries, a major cultural shift was underway in Europe. Intellectual currents that had prized reason and moderation during the Enlightenment gave way to new artistic and literary expressions emphasizing powerful emotion, individual creativity, and the sublime aspects of nature. This transition is often called the **Romantic Movement** (circa 1780s–1850s). In this chapter, we will explore how romantic ideals transformed understandings of love. We will see how leading poets, novelists, and philosophers championed passion, personal feeling, and the individual's subjective experience—redefining the cultural narrative around romantic relationships. We will also examine how political and social upheavals, like the French Revolution and the Napoleonic era, impacted the way love was portrayed and pursued.

1. HISTORICAL BACKDROP: REVOLUTIONARY ENERGY AND SOCIAL CHANGE

1.1 The French Revolution and Its Ripple Effects

At the close of the 18th century, the **French Revolution** (1789–1799) challenged many aspects of Europe's traditional order, from monarchy and aristocracy to church authority. Revolutionary ideals—**liberty, equality, fraternity**—promised a new social contract in which individual rights held paramount importance. Although the revolution soon descended into violence (the Reign of Terror) and complex power struggles, it showcased the possibility of radical social change.

This environment heightened individuals' sense that personal passions could drive collective transformations. The philosopher Jean-Jacques Rousseau's earlier emphasis on emotion and natural goodness found echoes in revolutionary discourse. People began to imagine that love, too, might be freed from older constraints—like arranged marriages or rigid class rules—if society reformed its institutions.

1.2 Romanticism as a Response to Rationalism

Romanticism emerged partly as a reaction against the Enlightenment's trust in reason and order. While Enlightenment thinkers had argued that knowledge and virtue were attained through calm, rational discourse, Romantics believed that some truths lay beyond rational comprehension—accessible instead through imagination, dreams, deep feeling, and communion with nature.

This outlook made them suspicious of the mechanistic view of human relationships. Instead of seeing love as a rational contract or a means to social stability, Romantic authors and artists praised love as a mysterious, intense, even chaotic force that could inspire artistic genius or heroic devotion. The Romantic Movement flourished in literature, painting, and music, celebrating individual expression and heartfelt passion. These values strongly influenced how people thought about courtship, marriage, and personal bonds.

2. ROMANTIC LITERATURE AND THE CULT OF PASSION

2.1 Key Romantic Writers and Their Influence

Romantic writers spanned diverse national traditions, but they shared certain themes. In Germany, **Johann Wolfgang von Goethe**'s early novel **"The Sorrows of Young Werther"** (1774) became a cultural phenomenon that prefigured the Romantic spirit. Werther's intense love for a woman betrothed to another man ends tragically, reflecting the romantic archetype of a sensitive soul overwhelmed by unrequited passion. Young men across Europe reportedly dressed like Werther, and some even tragically imitated his fate, revealing how powerfully a literary work could shape emotional ideals.

In England, poets like **William Wordsworth**, **Samuel Taylor Coleridge**, and **Lord Byron** gained fame for writing about nature, personal feeling, and rebellious individuality. Byron, in particular, personified the "Byronic hero"—a moody, passionate figure searching for unattainable ideals in love and life. **Percy Bysshe Shelley** and **John Keats** also wrote poems exalting the intensity of love, the fleeting nature of beauty, and the heartbreak that often accompanied deep emotion.

In France, **Alphonse de Lamartine** and later **Victor Hugo** contributed to Romantic verse and prose. Their works featured lovers battling social barriers or moral quandaries, with emotion portrayed as a powerful, even redemptive force.

In each of these contexts, romantic love was elevated to near-religious significance—transcending societal dictates, unafraid of heartbreak, and symbolic of a deeper quest for authenticity.

2.2 The Focus on Inner Emotions

Where earlier eras often framed love in external social terms—marriage alliances, moral duty, or companionate respect—Romantics placed the individual's inner emotional experience at the center of love. This shift encouraged the notion that the sincerity and depth of one's feelings mattered more than family expectations or religious mandates. A strong personal bond, heartfelt and passionate, could justify defying tradition if necessary.

Many Romantic narratives showed lovers pitted against societal norms: feuding families, class differences, or laws that forbade their union. The resulting tension underscored the Romantic belief that authentic feeling was a higher law than external convention. Readers responded strongly to these stories, identifying with characters who risked scandal or even death for love.

2.3 Nature as a Stage for Love

Romantics revered untamed landscapes—mountains, forests, or seas—as places where strong feelings could unfold free of social constraints. In poetry and novels, couples often found or lost each other in natural settings that symbolized their passion or turmoil. Stormy weather might reflect inner emotional storms; tranquil lakes might mirror harmonious love. This fascination with nature's sublimity paralleled the Romantics' view that love was an elemental force, akin to a rushing waterfall or raging tempest—beautiful, dangerous, and transformative.

Such depictions resonated in painting as well, with artists from the Romantic school portraying lone figures in vast landscapes, sometimes hinting at longing for a beloved or mourning lost affection. The environment became not just a backdrop but an active participant in the emotional narrative of love.

3. ROMANTIC LOVE IN DAILY LIFE

3.1 Middle-Class Aspirations and Literary Influence

While romantic literature often featured aristocratic or isolated heroes, it also shaped the expectations of the emerging middle class. People read popular novels or poems extolling the virtues of passionate, authentic attachment. Some individuals, especially younger readers, began to believe that true love should be a matter of intense feeling rather than social or economic convenience.

This did not instantly erase arranged marriages or parental authority. But diaries and letters from the early 19th century show more young men and women referencing literary ideals to advocate for personal choice. In some cases, families relented, allowing children to marry for love if the match was not too disadvantageous. Meanwhile, those who defied parental or community norms sometimes found a measure of cultural validation in Romantic themes that championed personal freedom over convention.

3.2 Love, Marriage, and Morality

Religious and civic institutions still governed moral standards, but the Romantic spirit introduced a new lens for judging relationships. An affair might be condemned by society but idealized in a novel if it seemed driven by a sincere, fated love. This tension between moral codes and romantic authenticity played out frequently in real life. Some men and women who faced loveless but socially approved matches felt torn between duty and the pursuit of genuine emotion.

Yet for all their exaltation of love, Romantics did not uniformly advocate promiscuity or disintegration of marriage norms. Many believed in the sanctity of a union based on affection and spiritual closeness. Adultery was still fraught with guilt and tragedy in Romantic stories—think of **Leo Tolstoy**'s later 19th-century novel *Anna Karenina*, which, while from a slightly later period, captures the Romantic legacy of love's power and its devastating potential consequences within a moral society.

3.3 Gender Roles in Romantic Partnerships

Women in Romantic literature often appear as objects of adoration or as muses who inspire male creativity. In real life, the idea that a woman could be her lover's "angel" or emotional anchor gained popularity, reinforcing a notion that women's purity and devotion were vital to a man's emotional growth. While this might seem like praise, it also confined women to roles centered on nurturing men's genius or feeling. They were rarely depicted as independent creators of their own destinies—though a few exceptions existed, like the poet **Caroline von Günderrode** in Germany or the novelist **Mary Shelley** in England, who explored themes of love, loss, and emotional complexity from a female viewpoint.

At the same time, many Romantic men were portrayed as tormented by love, grappling with existential despair. The archetype of the tortured male poet or restless wanderer in search of a higher ideal made intense emotional vulnerability acceptable for men, at least in the realm of literature. Real couples who identified with Romantic ideals might strive for a relationship in which both partners shared deep emotional intimacy, but the era's legal and social frameworks still placed men in positions of authority within marriage.

4. POLITICAL REVOLUTIONS AND LOVE

4.1 Napoleonic Era and Legal Codifications

The Napoleonic Wars (1803–1815) redrew Europe's political map, spreading French administrative systems, including the **Napoleonic Code**, into many regions. Introduced in 1804, the Napoleonic Code standardized laws on property, civil procedure, and family life in territories under French influence. It made civil marriage (performed by a state official) compulsory in France, marking a departure from exclusive church control. While it didn't revolve around Romantic ideals, it recognized marriage as a civil contract.

Nonetheless, the Code heavily favored paternal authority and restricted women's legal rights. It recognized divorce under certain conditions, but the process remained difficult, and women faced more stringent proof to obtain it than men. Thus, the tension between the Romantic emphasis on personal freedom in love and the legal reality of restricted choices for women persisted. Some couples who yearned for a freer union found the new laws only partly accommodating.

4.2 Revolutionary Ideals and Personal Choice

Outside of France, revolutionary fervor continued to flicker in various nationalist or liberal movements, occasionally linking the concept of personal liberty to the right to love and marry freely. Romantic nationalists, in places like Germany or Italy, wrote poems and songs equating romantic devotion to the love of a motherland. Personal and political passions merged, suggesting that the same spirit that fueled independence from foreign rule also drove individuals to defy social obstacles for love. This blending of romance and political idealism was seen in the life stories of revolutionary figures who formed relationships across cultural or class divides, though the results varied widely.

Romantic love, in this sense, could symbolize resistance to oppression—whether that oppression was tyrannical monarchy, parental dictates, or forced marriages. Yet real transformation of marriage customs happened slowly, as each region navigated the interplay between older traditions, Napoleonic reforms, and the Romantic aura of personal destiny.

5. THE MUSIC OF ROMANTIC PASSION

5.1 Beethoven and the Early Romantic Era

In classical music, **Ludwig van Beethoven** (1770–1827) straddled the line between the Classical and Romantic eras. His intense emotional style, especially in later works, influenced how people perceived the link between music and deep feeling. Though Beethoven's personal love life was complicated—he never married—letters and rumored dedications (like the "Immortal Beloved" letter) exemplified the Romantic trope of longing for an unattainable or idealized partner.

Romantic composers such as **Franz Schubert** in Austria or **Robert Schumann** in Germany wrote lieder (art songs) that centered on passionate yearnings, heartbreak, and the natural world as a mirror of human emotion. These songs, often set to Romantic poetry, gave a musical voice to private longing. Young people performing or listening to these pieces in salons or at small gatherings might feel that their own emotional experiences found an outlet in music's intimate power.

5.2 Opera in the Romantic Age

Building on the Baroque and Classical forms, 19th-century opera took romantic storylines to new levels of grandeur. Composers like **Gioachino Rossini**, **Gaetano Donizetti**, and **Vincenzo Bellini** in Italy crafted bel canto (beautiful singing) styles that featured passionate love arias and tragic scenarios. The hallmark of these works was the expression of raw human emotion through virtuosic vocal performance.

Later in the century, **Giuseppe Verdi** and **Richard Wagner** expanded opera's scope. Verdi's works—like *La Traviata*—explored the theme of love thwarted by social conventions, resonating with Romantic ideals of personal feeling in conflict with societal norms. Wagner's *Tristan und Isolde* famously depicted a love so potent it existed outside moral or rational bounds, culminating in a transcendent musical expression of longing and death. These operatic stories reinforced the notion that love was a force so profound it could break earthly constraints, consistent with Romantic emphasis on the sublime intensity of the heart.

6. THE GOTHIC ELEMENT AND DARK ROMANCE

6.1 Gothic Novels and Forbidden Love

A sub-genre of Romantic literature, the **Gothic novel**, thrived in Britain and spread to other countries. Authors such as **Ann Radcliffe**, **Matthew Lewis** (*The Monk*), and later **Charles Maturin** penned tales set in crumbling castles or eerie landscapes, featuring secrets, supernatural hints, and intense emotional states. Love often appeared as a perilous, thrilling encounter with the unknown—a pure-hearted heroine pursued by a mysterious or menacing figure. While these novels entertained with horror elements, they also explored the darker side of passion: obsession, madness, and moral ambiguity.

This Gothic dimension extended the Romantic fascination with extremes of feeling. Readers devoured stories where romantic desire was tinged with danger, moral conflict, or the presence of ghosts. In personal diaries, some individuals wrote about the "Gothic" flair in their own relationships, likening emotional storms to the storms in Radcliffe's novels. The result was a cultural atmosphere where love was both revered and feared, recognized as a potent force that could lead to ecstasy or doom.

6.2 Byronic Heroes and Fatal Attraction

Lord Byron (1788–1824), with his "Byronic hero," epitomized the darker side of Romantic love. The Byronic hero was brooding, flawed, often haunted by a secret guilt or cursed destiny. Byron's poems, like *Childe Harold's Pilgrimage* or the dramatic narrative *Manfred*, portrayed men who roamed exotic locales, scornful of society, longing for a love that might redeem them but rarely finding lasting peace.

This archetype resonated widely. Young men identifying with the Byronic hero might adopt a manner of moody introspection, seeing themselves as doomed lovers misunderstood by a conformist world. In real relationships, a "Byronic" stance could produce tumultuous entanglements. Some women were drawn to the mystique of a rebellious, tormented lover, while others found it dangerously self-absorbed. The cultural fascination with such figures reveals how Romanticism could glorify intense, and sometimes destructive, love.

7. REALITY CHECK: SOCIAL STRUCTURES AND LIMITS OF ROMANTIC IDEALS

7.1 Continued Arranged Marriages and Class Barriers

Despite the fervor for passionate unions, traditional marriage practices persisted. Among nobility, families often arranged matches to preserve titles and lands. Merchant dynasties likewise sought alliances that benefited business prospects. Even in middle-class families, parents might guide or pressure children to marry suitably. Romantic love was sometimes indulged as a polite pastime—harmless so long as it did not challenge vital social or economic interests.

For couples who truly wanted to marry purely for love, crossing class lines was still fraught with risk. **Honor** remained a powerful concept, particularly for aristocrats. A daughter running off with a lower-status man could face disinheritance or exile. The cultural conversation about love as an ennobling force existed, but it coexisted with stark social realities. Many Romantic novels themselves ended in tragedy, underscoring how rarely unbridled passion overcame entrenched barriers.

7.2 Sexuality and Morality

Public morality in the early 19th century varied regionally. Some conservative societies—like parts of Germany or rural France—still held strong church influence, condemning premarital relations. But in cities, an undercurrent of freer behavior among Bohemians or artistic circles sometimes clashed with bourgeois respectability. Writers might celebrate the raw honesty of sexual desire, but official norms and legal codes typically penalized adultery or "lewd" behavior, especially for women.

Romanticism's glorification of intense passion did not always align with prudish social customs. Secret affairs, divorces, or open cohabitation occasionally happened in avant-garde circles. However, these choices risked social ostracism. Women faced greater repercussions than men if they broke marital vows or engaged in scandalous conduct. This double standard carried over from previous centuries, though the Romantic ethos of individual feeling spurred some men and women to challenge hypocrisy.

8. WOMEN WRITERS AND THE FEMALE PERSPECTIVE

8.1 Female Novelists in the Romantic Era

While many female authors remained overshadowed by male contemporaries, some gained fame and contributed significantly to the Romantic discourse on love. In England, **Jane Austen** (1775–1817) wrote novels like *Pride and Prejudice* (1813) and *Sense and Sensibility* (1811), blending a rational perspective with a recognition of emotional needs. Though often classified more as "Regency" than high Romantic, Austen's works revolve around courtship, exploring how love and marriage intersect with economic security and social reputation. Her heroines, though witty and independent-minded, still function within a patriarchal world, revealing the tension between personal inclination and social demands.

Mary Shelley (1797–1851), best known for *Frankenstein* (1818), engaged with Romantic themes of creation, ambition, and the consequences of uncontrolled passion. In her personal life, she eloped with the poet Percy Bysshe Shelley—a bold, rebellious act reflecting Romantic ideals. Her writings occasionally touched on love's redemptive or destructive capacities. Another figure, **Charlotte Brontë** (1816–1855), though slightly later in the Victorian era, showcased the Romantic spirit in *Jane Eyre* (1847), where the heroine's quest for love coexists with moral self-respect.

8.2 New Depths of Female Emotional Agency

These women authors, along with others less known to history, gave female characters greater depth. Rather than being mere muses or moral ornaments, heroines wrestled with their own desires, moral judgments, and social constraints. A few had the boldness to resist an unwanted marriage or to follow a forbidden love—though typically with caution. This literary representation of women as active emotional beings, capable of heartbreak and moral reasoning, paved the way for future feminist developments, albeit in a slow, uneven manner.

9. ROMANTIC ART, LANDSCAPE, AND LOVE

9.1 Romantic Painters

In visual art, Romantic painters used intense color, dramatic light, and emotive brushstrokes to convey states of mind. **Eugène Delacroix** in France depicted revolutionary struggles, mythic scenes, and subjects brimming with passion. Works like *The Death of Sardanapalus* showcased love and desire entangled with violence and tragedy. Meanwhile, in Britain, **J.M.W. Turner** and **John Constable** created landscapes that, while not always directly illustrating love stories, evoked moods of longing or serenity that paralleled Romantic literary themes. A couple might be placed as tiny figures in a vast, majestic setting—symbolizing how personal love can be dwarfed or intensified by the grandeur of nature.

9.2 The Sublime and Human Feeling

Romantic art often celebrated the **sublime**—the awe-inspiring aspects of nature or existence that surpass normal human control. Artists found resonance with love as equally sublime: an overwhelming force that could transport individuals beyond mundane reality. In portrayals of lovers meeting on a storm-swept cliff or parted by a raging sea, the environment acted as a metaphor for emotional extremes. This synergy between nature's grandeur and the lovers' passions exemplified a Romantic worldview, suggesting that true love is as boundless, unpredictable, and awe-striking as the wildest landscapes.

10. LEGACY AND CONCLUSION

10.1 The Romantic Movement's Impact on Cultural Norms

Romanticism left a powerful imprint on how Western societies perceived love. The idea that personal, heartfelt emotion could override rational calculations, social hierarchies, or even moral strictures became widely accepted in cultural consciousness. Though arranged marriages and legal inequalities persisted, the notion that love should be the prime mover in marriage gained substantial ground. Younger generations found in Romantic literature a blueprint for self-determined passion, fueling countless elopements or clandestine affairs. The tension between passion and society became a defining narrative for the 19th century.

Simultaneously, Romantic art, music, and literature offered intense portrayals of love's triumphs and tragedies, influencing subsequent creative movements. The Romantic hero or heroine—torn by longing, scorning convention—endured in Western culture, setting the stage for modern depictions of rebellious lovers in film, novels, and popular music centuries later.

10.2 Connecting Romanticism to Later Developments

By the mid-19th century, Romanticism itself began evolving. Industrialization, social reform movements, and new scientific theories prompted fresh debates about the place of emotion and imagination. Some critics saw Romantic love as naive or unproductive in a rapidly modernizing world. Others, however, championed it as an antidote to the dehumanizing aspects of industrial society.

The ideals of self-realization and emotional authenticity in relationships would continue to inform the later 19th-century movements, including **Realism** in literature and the eventual **Victorian** moral climate, which absorbed and reshaped Romantic impulses in distinct ways. Even as society demanded outward respectability, Romantic notions of personal feeling quietly thrived under the surface. As we proceed to **Chapter 19: The Victorian Age and Love**, we will see how the 19th century's second half wove Romantic legacies into a rigid social fabric—balancing strict moral codes with a deep undercurrent of passion, secrecy, and the continued quest for genuine emotional fulfillment.

CHAPTER 19

THE VICTORIAN AGE AND LOVE

With the ascendance of **Queen Victoria** to the British throne in 1837, a new era began, lasting until her death in 1901. The **Victorian Age** symbolizes much more than just British history; it reflects broader 19th-century Western developments in morality, technology, imperial expansion, and social norms. This period is often remembered for a contrast between outward propriety and an undercurrent of intense emotion or desire—especially in matters of love and marriage. In this chapter, we will explore how Victorian values shaped romantic relationships, how the Industrial Revolution changed social life, and how literature and art of the time grappled with the conflicts between respectability, passion, and emerging challenges to traditional gender roles.

1. HISTORICAL CONTEXT: INDUSTRIALIZATION AND SOCIAL ORDER

1.1 The Industrial Revolution

During the Victorian era (and similar time frames in other European countries and the United States), the **Industrial Revolution** reached new heights. Factories, railways, and urbanization transformed the landscape, drawing millions into rapidly growing cities. Middle-class entrepreneurs prospered, while working-class laborers faced harsh conditions. This shift in economic power further eroded the old feudal hierarchy, increasing the social influence of business families who prized discipline, respectability, and stable domestic life.

For love and marriage, this meant a growing emphasis on the home as a moral haven away from the tumult of industrial capitalism. **Separate spheres** ideology took hold: men dealt with the competitive public sphere (business, politics), while women were expected to cultivate the private sphere of home and family. Romantic love fit neatly into this domestic ideal, though it was bounded by strict moral codes that prized chastity, fidelity, and outward decorum.

1.2 The Spread of Victorian Morality

While "Victorian" is rooted in British history, many Western societies adopted or shared similar moral attitudes in the mid-to-late 19th century. Modesty, self-control, and social conformity were valued. Middle-class families, in particular, strove to present a virtuous image, policing their members' behavior. Church attendance remained common; religious revivals in various denominations reinforced biblical models of marriage and sexual morality.

Nonetheless, the Romantic legacy persisted. People still desired emotional closeness in marriage, and novels or poems still celebrated deep passion. But open displays of sexuality or deviance were taboo. Couples might yearn for a heartfelt bond while navigating a minefield of social rules. The push for respectability fueled a culture of discretion: if illicit affairs occurred, they were concealed carefully to avoid scandal that could ruin a family's standing.

2. VICTORIAN COURTSHIP AND MARRIAGE RITUALS

2.1 Elaborate Etiquette and Social Events

Victorian courtship, especially among the middle and upper classes, followed a formal script. Young women were "presented" to society at balls or gatherings once they reached a suitable age—often their late teens. Gentlemen sought introductions through mutual acquaintances; direct approach was considered improper. Chaperones frequently accompanied unmarried women to ensure that any interactions with men remained respectable. Couples might exchange polite conversation at dances or dinner parties, where each gesture or compliment held significance.

Calling cards became an essential part of social life. A man would leave his card at a young woman's home, signaling interest. If the family approved, he might be invited for a daytime visit in the drawing room, still under watchful supervision. Engagements were often short once a couple agreed—delaying marriage risked rumors of impropriety. During the engagement, public displays of affection were minimal: perhaps a brief walk together or discreet letters. The wedding itself showcased not just a private union but the family's social status, with elaborate ceremonies and receptions.

2.2 Role of Parents and Economic Considerations

While some Victorian novels romanticize love matches, parental influence remained strong. Families screened suitors for financial stability, character, and social background. Middle-class parents worried about a daughter marrying a man who lacked secure prospects or moral uprightness. In aristocratic circles, dynastic ambitions still played a role. Indeed, "love matches" often had to align with property or inheritance concerns, though the ideal scenario was that a suitable suitor also won the bride's affections.

Dowries or settlements were common. A father might provide a sum to support his daughter's future household, while the groom's family guaranteed an inheritance or a share in a business. These practicalities did not necessarily negate love, but they added a financial dimension to marriage negotiations. When love and economics conflicted, some couples eloped—though that carried stigma. For working-class people, marriage was often postponed until a man's wages could support a household; genuine affection might exist, but survival needs shaped timing and choice.

2.3 Married Life and Domestic Ideals

Once married, women were expected to focus on home management, childrearing, and moral guidance. Husbands handled external affairs but were urged to show kindness and not succumb to vices like gambling or extramarital temptations. Middle-class publications glorified the **"angel in the house"** model—taken from a popular 19th-century poem—portraying the wife as pure, selfless, and eternally devoted. This placed enormous pressure on women to maintain a serene household.

Love, within this framework, was sentimental yet contained. Demonstrations of devotion might be expressed through small gestures: a husband bringing a gift from town, a wife sewing a personal item, or shared reading by the fireside. Public or passionate displays were discouraged, as Victorian codes demanded modesty. Yet diaries from the period reveal that many couples did share deep affection, with wives sometimes writing ardent entries about their husbands' virtues and husbands describing a tender bond that gave them solace from a stressful public life.

3. GENDER ROLES AND CONSTRAINTS

3.1 The Doctrine of Separate Spheres

The concept of **"separate spheres"** allocated distinct realms for men and women. Men inhabited the world of commerce, politics, and intellectual debate, while women presided over domestic life, moral upbringing, and emotional warmth. This ideology drew on earlier ideas but reached its zenith in the Victorian era. Love was framed as a gentle, civilizing force that women introduced to men's otherwise competitive environment.

However, this separation reinforced women's dependence. Without legal or financial autonomy, wives were vulnerable if a marriage turned abusive or if a husband squandered resources. Divorce remained extremely difficult. In Britain, the **Matrimonial Causes Act of 1857** introduced a civil divorce court, but double standards prevailed: a husband could cite simple adultery, while a wife had to prove adultery compounded by cruelty or desertion to obtain a divorce. Thus, though "romantic love" was championed as a basis for marriage, society provided few escape routes for women if that love died.

3.2 Sexual Morality and the Double Standard

Victorian society placed stringent expectations on female chastity, both before and within marriage. A "fallen woman"—one who engaged in premarital or extramarital relations—faced harsh condemnation. Men, on the other hand, were not always held to the same standard. While extramarital affairs were publicly frowned upon, men's "indiscretions" were sometimes overlooked if discreet. Prostitution flourished in Victorian cities, catering to men's desires while the official moral code deemed such acts sinful.

This contradiction fueled debates among reformers. Some voices, including religious and philanthropic groups, campaigned against the exploitation of prostitutes and called for men to uphold the same purity demanded of women. Yet the culture of secrecy prevailed. Many middle-class wives, unaware or powerless, simply hoped their husbands remained faithful. The romantic rhetoric of mutual devotion coexisted with a social reality that often penalized only one side for moral lapses.

3.3 Women's Movements and Early Feminist Critiques

A growing number of women recognized the inequality. Figures like **John Stuart Mill**, though male, argued in works like *The Subjection of Women* (1869) that legal and social barriers to women's equality were unjust. Women activists, some from the educated middle class, began pushing for reforms—property rights for married women, custody rights to children, and eventually voting rights. Writers like **Elizabeth Barrett Browning** expressed strong emotional and intellectual partnership in their marriages, as seen in her Sonnets from the Portuguese, which highlight a woman poet's voice in love.

Still, structural change was slow. Many Victorians could not imagine upending the separate spheres. Even women who championed female education often believed in the moral superiority of women's domestic role. Yet the seeds of broader emancipation were planted, partly motivated by the contradiction between the romantic notion of equal love and the actual subordination of wives under the law.

4. LITERARY REFLECTIONS OF LOVE IN THE VICTORIAN AGE

4.1 The Novel as a Mirror of Courtship

The Victorian era saw a boom in novel-writing. Authors like **Charles Dickens**, **William Makepeace Thackeray**, and **George Eliot** (Mary Ann Evans) portrayed a range of social classes and moral dilemmas. Love stories threaded through these narratives, capturing how men and women navigated societal pressures. **Dickens** often combined love plots with social critique—*David Copperfield* (1850) includes multiple courtships, revealing how innocence or cunning can shape romantic fates.

George Eliot tackled deeper psychological aspects in works like *Middlemarch* (1871–72). Characters form marriages that test their aspirations. Some marry for idealistic visions of mutual purpose; others discover love marred by mismatched goals. Eliot's nuanced portrayal suggests love is not only a private feeling but also shaped by personal growth, moral duty, and social constraints. Her heroines, like Dorothea Brooke, combine a yearning for intellectual companionship with a sense of philanthropic or spiritual calling, reflecting the complexity of Victorian moral landscapes.

4.2 Sensational and Gothic Threads

Apart from realistic novels, the **sensation novel** emerged in the 1860s, featuring bigamy, madness, and hidden identities within seemingly respectable households. Authors like **Wilkie Collins** (*The Woman in White*, 1859-60) showed how love could entangle innocent protagonists in sinister plots. This sub-genre blended Romantic intensity with Victorian moral anxiety, thrilling readers with scandal while ultimately restoring conventional virtue.

Gothic elements also persisted. **Charlotte Brontë**'s *Jane Eyre* (1847) straddles Romantic and Victorian styles, presenting a heroine who insists on moral and emotional equality in love. Mr. Rochester, with his dark secrets and moody temperament, recalls the Byronic hero. But Jane, though plain and without fortune, asserts her dignity, demanding a partnership of equals—a quietly revolutionary stance for the time. This interplay of passion, integrity, and social critique epitomizes how Victorian authors explored love's possibilities within moral strictures.

4.3 Poetry: Tension Between Restraint and Ardor

Victorian poets also grappled with love themes. **Alfred, Lord Tennyson** wrote lyrical verse extolling devotion—*In Memoriam* A.H.H. (1850) dealt with grief for a friend, but Tennyson's works also touched on romantic fidelity. The Brownings—**Robert Browning** and **Elizabeth Barrett Browning**—became literary icons of a poetically minded couple. Elizabeth's *Sonnets from the Portuguese* revealed intense personal love that soared beyond typical Victorian reserve, though she cloaked them in a foreign title to appear less self-exposing.

Poetry often walked a fine line: celebrating emotional depth while maintaining a modest or moral facade. Some verses used nature imagery—hearkening to Romantic tradition—to suggest love's power. Others employed religious or classical references to elevate love above mere passion. The tension between wanting to depict strong desire and needing to fit a respectable Victorian mold shaped the era's poetic expression.

5. THE ROLE OF PRINT CULTURE AND MASS READING

5.1 Expansion of Readership

Mass literacy grew rapidly in the 19th century, supported by compulsory education in some nations and cheaper printing methods. Women, in particular, became a large segment of the reading public. Novels about love or domestic life found a receptive audience, influencing how real people imagined their own courtships. Advice columns, women's magazines, and etiquette manuals proliferated, instructing readers on everything from how to exchange calling cards to maintaining a virtuous engagement.

While these texts reinforced conventional morality, they also validated the yearning for personal fulfillment in marriage. The ability to read widely gave both men and women new role models—heroines defying ill-suited suitors or heroes proving devotion through adversity. Some readers found resonance in these fictional arcs and tried to apply them to real relationships, resulting in a subtle interplay between literature and lived experience.

5.2 Advice Manuals and Moral Guidance

Conduct books and **marriage guides** aimed to shape behavior. They advised wives to be patient, gentle, and impeccably moral, ensuring a tranquil home that would keep a husband away from vices. Husbands were urged to be firm but kind, protecting wives from coarse aspects of business or politics. These manuals often highlighted the importance of mutual love as the bedrock of a Christian household, though always underscored that love must remain within the boundaries of social respectability.

For young couples, the advice typically included caution about unrestrained passion. Emotional closeness was good, but too much fervor could threaten self-control. Thus, Victorian love was supposed to be warm but disciplined, heartfelt but never "improper." The overall message: love was integral to marriage, but it must be channeled responsibly to uphold family and societal order.

6. SEXUALITY AND THE "PRIVATE VICE, PUBLIC VIRTUE" DYNAMIC

6.1 Prostitution and the Underworld

While Victorian moral codes prescribed chastity for unmarried women and fidelity within marriage, a large subculture of prostitution thrived in major cities. Men's demand for sexual services outside official moral norms coexisted with a facade of respectability. Social reformers like **Josephine Butler** campaigned against the Contagious Diseases Acts, which attempted to regulate prostitution by forcibly examining women suspected of venereal disease. Butler and others called out the hypocrisy of punishing female prostitutes while ignoring male clients who broke the same moral standards.

Thus, a double standard allowed men to indulge in "private vice" while society insisted on "public virtue." Wives might suspect or even know about their husbands' visits to brothels, but they had limited recourse. The tension between romantic ideals of monogamous love and the reality of extramarital arrangements was a defining paradox of the age.

6.2 Illegitimacy and Fallen Women Narratives

Falling pregnant out of wedlock carried enormous stigma. Single mothers received little sympathy; many ended up in poverty or forced to give children to foundling hospitals. Novels like **Thomas Hardy**'s *Tess of the d'Urbervilles* (1891), though slightly post-Victorian, illustrate a woman's ruin following sexual exploitation and societal judgment. Earlier in the century, authors seldom tackled such themes openly, but sensational or "social problem" novels occasionally depicted the harsh fate of a "fallen" woman.

Such stories underscored the precariousness of women's social standing. Romantic love gone wrong could destroy a woman's life if it led to a scandal. Even within marriage, wives who suspected husbands' unfaithfulness typically had no legal grounds to separate unless severe cruelty was proven. Thus, Victorian society's emphasis on modesty and moral purity could produce tragic outcomes for those who strayed from the idealized path.

7. CROSS-CULTURAL ENCOUNTERS AND COLONIAL INFLUENCES

7.1 Love in the Context of Empire

Victorian Britain was the center of a vast empire, and European powers generally were expanding colonial rule worldwide. Administrators, soldiers, and traders lived for years in colonies like India or Africa. Their letters and memoirs sometimes describe relationships with local women, ranging from official marriages (rarely recognized back home) to unofficial arrangements or exploitative liaisons. The racially charged ideology of empire complicated these attachments, as families in Europe often disapproved of "mixed" matches.

Simultaneously, certain colonial administrators or missionaries urged "civilizing" local populations, including pushing Victorian marital ideals on societies with different customs. In places like India, legislation influenced by British reformers altered local marriage practices, raising the age of consent, for example. These interventions sparked debates about whether European moral norms or local traditions should prevail. Love, marriage, and family became flashpoints in colonial contexts, reflecting a clash of cultural values.

7.2 Exoticism and Romantic Fantasies

Back in Europe, popular literature sometimes exoticized colonial locales, weaving romantic or tragic tales of cross-cultural love. Some Victorian stories depicted a European man and a "native" woman parted by incompatible traditions—mirroring older Romantic tropes about love defying boundaries. However, these narratives often reinforced stereotypes of the "mysterious East" or "noble savage," rarely granting genuine agency to the indigenous partner. Real unions that bridged cultural differences remained a minority phenomenon, typically overshadowed by prejudice or the weight of imperial power structures.

8. ADVANCES IN SCIENCE, PSYCHOLOGY, AND THEIR IMPACT ON LOVE

8.1 Early Psychology and Emotional Understanding

By the late 19th century, scientific advances in physiology and embryonic psychology began probing human behavior. While not yet a fully developed field, researchers and physicians studied hysteria, sexuality, and emotional disorders. Some applied evolutionary theory—sparked by **Charles Darwin**'s work—to social relationships, arguing that love might be tied to reproductive advantage or survival instincts.

Though these ideas were preliminary, they opened the door to seeing love not only as a spiritual or moral phenomenon but as a subject for empirical investigation. Writers like **Herbert Spencer** or early sexologists in Germany (e.g., Richard von Krafft-Ebing) proposed that human affection had biological underpinnings. This approach sometimes conflicted with Victorian moral codes but foreshadowed 20th-century psychological theories that would delve deeper into desire, attachment, and emotional development.

8.2 Controversies Over Birth Control and Eugenics

Discrete discussions of birth control began cropping up, though publicly taboo. Activists like **Annie Besant** or **Charles Bradlaugh** in Britain championed the right to publish information about contraception, facing obscenity charges. They argued that controlling reproduction could enhance marital love by freeing couples from endless pregnancies. Opponents insisted that such knowledge promoted immorality. Meanwhile, early eugenic ideas twisted Darwinian concepts into arguments about "improving" the human race, sometimes advocating selective marriage or childbearing—a notion that would have disturbing consequences in the next century.

These debates signaled cracks in the monolithic Victorian worldview. Love and marriage were still celebrated as moral and respectable, but the ways couples approached intimacy and reproduction were subtly shifting, hinting at transformations that would accelerate in the 20th century.

9. LATE VICTORIAN CHALLENGES AND TRANSITIONS

9.1 The New Woman and Emergent Modernity

Toward the century's end, a figure known as the **"New Woman"** appeared in literature and social commentary. These were women who sought higher education, engaged in professions (teaching, nursing, journalism), and advocated for suffrage. Their more independent stance on marriage—insisting they might remain single or choose a partner for love and mutual respect—troubled traditionalists who feared the collapse of family order.

In fiction, authors like **Thomas Hardy**, **George Gissing**, and **Sarah Grand** presented heroines who chafed at conventional marriage. They wanted personal fulfillment, intellectual companionship, or simpler equality. Some found love that recognized their aspirations; others faced tragedy in a society unready for such transformations. The tension between the romantic dream of unity and the reality of patriarchal constraints became a major theme in late Victorian narratives.

9.2 Shifts in Popular Culture

Popular culture also signaled incremental changes. Music halls in urban areas featured comedic or sentimental songs about love, sometimes with more frank references to courtship challenges. Middle-class families might attend the theater or read serialized novels that poked gentle fun at outdated parental interference. Meanwhile, traveling circuses or fairs provided chances for young people of different backgrounds to meet outside strict chaperoned environments. Though the moral climate stayed conservative, pockets of freer social interaction emerged, especially in bustling cities where anonymity was possible.

The bicycle craze of the 1890s, for instance, allowed women some physical mobility—riding unaccompanied, wearing more practical attire, and occasionally courting while cycling with a suitor. While hardly a revolution, these small shifts eroded older patterns, letting romantic contact happen with less direct parental oversight. Even so, scandal could ensue if a woman's behavior seemed too bold, illustrating how Victorian society clung to its codes despite underlying changes.

10. CONCLUSION

The Victorian Age refined and complicated the ideals of love inherited from earlier centuries. Publicly, it elevated marriage as a morally upright, emotionally warm, but carefully regulated institution. Courtship rituals—like calling cards, chaperoned visits, and formal engagements—sought to preserve decorum. Once married, couples were expected to embody domestic virtue, with the wife as a nurturing "angel" and the husband as a benevolent provider.

Beneath this surface, paradoxes abounded. The same society that praised moral fidelity often tolerated male infidelity while condemning women harshly for any sexual slip. The romantic quest for heartfelt companionship, championed by novelists and poets, had to contend with the reality of women's limited legal rights and men's predominant social power. Yet the idea of marriage as a union based on genuine affection and mutual respect became deeply entrenched in mainstream consciousness.

By the turn of the 20th century, signs of transition multiplied. Feminist movements, rising secularism, urban anonymity, and expanding print culture all eroded the absolute hold of Victorian norms. The era's legacy would continue to shape modern love, forming a foundation of moral respectability that later generations would question or redefine. As we move into **Chapter 20: Early 20th Century Perspectives on Love**, we will see how world wars, psychological theories, and further social upheavals disrupted Victorian traditions and propelled love into the complexities of the modern age.

CHAPTER 20

EARLY 20TH CENTURY PERSPECTIVES ON LOVE

As the 20th century dawned, the world was on the brink of rapid transformation. In many places, the Victorian moral framework still lingered, but fresh winds of change—social, political, and intellectual—promised to reshape ideas about love and relationships. This chapter looks at the opening decades of the 1900s, before the full onset of modernity, to understand how love was perceived, practiced, and challenged. We will see how new psychological theories, the rise of women's movements, changing courtship norms, and the disruptions of world conflicts gradually steered society away from Victorian traditions and toward a more modern concept of emotional bonds.

1. HISTORICAL CONTEXT: A NEW CENTURY DAWNS

1.1 The End of an Era and the Seeds of Modernity

When Queen Victoria died in 1901, her passing symbolically closed the Victorian Age. Yet her influence persisted in many countries, especially in former colonies of the British Empire and in nations that had borrowed Victorian moral codes. At the same time, industrialization continued apace, fueling urban growth and labor migrations. Women demanded greater autonomy, reformers criticized social inequalities, and breakthroughs in science questioned long-held assumptions.

In cultural terms, new artistic movements (Impressionism, Post-Impressionism, Early Modernism) reflected a growing willingness to discard conventional forms. Writers experimented with stream-of-consciousness narratives, while avant-garde groups explored symbolism, expressionism, or futurism. Against this backdrop, personal relationships came under fresh scrutiny. People began to challenge whether the old, rigid codes of courtship and marriage could meet the needs of a rapidly changing society.

1.2 Social Tensions and Political Shifts

Early 20th-century Europe was rife with tensions. Empires like Austro-Hungary and Ottoman Turkey faced nationalist stirrings. In many Western countries, socialist or labor movements clamored for workers' rights, often intersecting with questions of women's role in the workforce and at home. Meanwhile, the upper classes strove to maintain stability, sometimes clinging to older moral norms about marriage and family. As new nations or movements formed, the concept of "love" as a private emotion jostled with the reality of ongoing class struggles, political rivalries, and the looming possibility of war.

In the United States, the "Progressive Era" (circa 1890s–1920s) paralleled these developments, tackling social reforms and expanding women's suffrage. Love and marriage in America mirrored European patterns but also had distinct features—like the influence of frontier culture, diverse immigrant communities, and a robust popular entertainment industry that began shaping romantic ideals through music, theater, and later motion pictures. By 1914, with the outbreak of World War I, the world would enter a period of upheaval that profoundly impacted personal lives and romantic possibilities.

2. WOMEN'S EMANCIPATION MOVEMENTS AND LOVE

2.1 Suffragettes and the Demand for Equality

In the first decades of the 20th century, women's suffrage campaigns gained momentum in Britain, the United States, and elsewhere. Activists like **Emmeline Pankhurst** in Britain led public protests and hunger strikes, demanding the right to vote. Their actions challenged the idea that a woman's role was purely domestic. Meanwhile, in the U.S., leaders like **Susan B. Anthony**, **Elizabeth Cady Stanton**, and **Alice Paul** continued the push for women's political participation.

Though the immediate goal was voting rights, these movements also carried implications for romantic relationships. Greater political engagement hinted that women could assert themselves not only in the public sphere but also in private decision-making about suitors, marriage, and family planning. The notion of "companionate marriage," already floated in the 19th century, now intersected with demands that a wife be recognized as a full citizen with legal personhood. If love was to be an equal partnership, then the broader society needed to treat men and women as equals, at least in theory.

2.2 Early Feminist Thinkers on Love and Marriage

Writers such as **Charlotte Perkins Gilman** in the U.S. argued that the economic dependence of wives stunted real partnership. In her book *The Home: Its Work and Influence* (1903), Gilman proposed that housework be professionalized or socialized, freeing women to develop personal talents and share in broader civic responsibilities. She believed that if a marriage was built on genuine affection, neither partner should be subordinate. Others, like **Emma Goldman**, an anarchist thinker, took a more radical stance, criticizing marriage as a patriarchal institution that stifled women's potential. She championed free unions grounded in mutual love without state or church sanction, though such views were widely considered scandalous.

Still, mainstream society remained wary of these calls for sweeping reform. Most couples continued to marry within the older framework, though some adopted small changes: couples might negotiate roles, wives might take on part-time work, or spouses might discuss issues of birth control more openly. The seeds of a new emotional dynamic were there, but legal and cultural inertia kept transformations slow.

2.3 The Nexus of Courtship, Freedom, and Respectability

For unmarried women who joined the workforce in shops, factories, or offices, the experience of earning a wage and interacting with male colleagues gave them more social autonomy. They might engage in "dating" (a term gaining use in the U.S.) that involved less chaperoning. Yet respectability still demanded caution: a woman who appeared too bold could face gossip or risk her reputation. The tension between personal freedom and communal judgment remained potent. Some women found a delicate balance by partaking in new social activities—like dance halls or amusement parks—without blatantly defying moral codes. Love, thus, was in flux, caught between the desire for self-determination and the weight of customary decorum.

3. RISE OF PSYCHOLOGY AND NEW INSIGHTS INTO HUMAN DESIRE

3.1 Sigmund Freud and the Exploration of Sexuality

One of the most influential figures of the early 20th century was **Sigmund Freud** (1856–1939). His theories about the unconscious mind, libido, and the formative impact of childhood experiences changed how Western societies talked about love and sexuality. In works like *Three Essays on the Theory of Sexuality* (1905), Freud argued that sexual desire was fundamental to human behavior, influencing not only procreation but also creativity, neuroses, and emotional bonds.

Freud's notion that repressed desires could cause mental distress challenged Victorian taboos about open discussion of sexuality. While his concepts were controversial and not universally accepted, they found a growing audience among intellectuals. Couples and individuals began to question whether stifling one's sexual urges or idealizing romantic love might lead to psychological complications. Therapists, psychoanalysts, and popular writers started referencing Freud to explain everything from marital dissatisfaction to the complexities of courtship. Gradually, this "talking cure" culture chipped away at the old reticence surrounding physical and emotional intimacy.

3.2 Other Psychological Theories and Relationship Advice

Freud was not alone. Thinkers like **Carl Jung** and later psychoanalysts proposed alternative or complementary ideas about the unconscious and archetypes, affecting how people viewed relationships. Early social psychologists examined courtship behaviors, attraction, and emotional attachments, though still in embryonic form. Advice books on love and marriage increasingly borrowed psychological terminology, telling readers to "understand their partner's psyche" or "resolve hidden conflicts" rather than just follow moral instructions.

These shifts did not instantly revolutionize how couples behaved, but they introduced a new language: one in which love was not merely moral or sentimental but also psychological, with layers of hidden desire and potential trauma. The revelation that romantic feelings might have deep, often unconscious roots made love both more intriguing and more precarious.

4. CHANGING COURTSHIP PRACTICES: FROM FORMALITY TO INFORMALITY

4.1 The Emergence of "Dating" in Urban Centers

In the U.S., the term "dating" began to describe a more casual meeting of potential partners. Instead of formal courtship under parental watch, young people in cities might visit dance halls, movie theaters (nickelodeons early on), or soda fountains. The anonymity of large urban environments allowed them to experiment with social interactions that were less strictly policed. While the middle classes still valued propriety, a growing youth culture embraced these new freedoms.

In Europe, similar patterns emerged in metropolitan areas like Paris, Berlin, or Vienna. Cafés, cabarets, and dance venues offered semi-public spaces for flirtation. This was not a universal phenomenon—many rural or conservative communities retained old-fashioned betrothal customs—but it signaled a gradual shift. The concept of love as a private choice, fueled by mutual attraction rather than parental arrangement, gained traction among younger generations.

4.2 Technological Advances and Communication

The spread of the telephone and improved postal services enabled swifter, more private communication between potential lovers. While letters had long been part of courtship, the telephone allowed immediate conversations, albeit often with other household members in earshot. Motorized transport—trains, buses, early automobiles—let couples travel for picnics or outings unchaperoned, offering personal space away from home. These small freedoms eroded the rigid Victorian model, inching society toward a more relaxed approach to romantic engagement.

Still, concerns about "decency" persisted. Parents worried about unsupervised outings leading to physical intimacy or moral lapses. Reformers published warnings about the dangers of dance halls or jazz clubs, which they claimed encouraged sinful behavior. Anxieties about youth losing respect for tradition indicated the cultural growing pains as love moved from structured social ritual to more autonomous, emotionally driven relationships.

5. POPULAR CULTURE AND THE ROMANCE MEDIA

5.1 Silent Cinema and Idealized Love

The early film industry, especially in places like the U.S. (Hollywood) and Europe (Pathé in France, UFA in Germany), produced silent movies that often featured romantic plots. Stars such as **Rudolph Valentino** cultivated a screen image of the passionate lover, influencing public fantasies about courtship. Films like *The Sheik* (1921) depicted exotic, swooning romance, feeding viewers' dreams of intense, dramatic love far removed from daily constraints.

While many of these plots were simplistic, they contributed to a collective cultural narrative where love was an adventure, transcending social barriers. Young fans might swoon over film idols, adopting fashions or mannerisms that signaled a longing for a similarly passionate love. Some moral guardians denounced this cinematic influence, fearing it taught unrealistic or immoral lessons. Yet the popularity of romantic films underscored how hungry the public was for stories about personal choice and emotional intensity.

5.2 Magazines and Love Stories

Magazines targeting women flourished, printing serialized romance stories and advice columns. They offered tips on grooming, letter-writing, and managing suitors, occasionally including more daring pieces about the importance of mutual pleasure or understanding. Some columns encouraged women to be discerning, to seek a partner who respected their interests and intellect, echoing the push for greater female autonomy.

Readers wrote letters to these periodicals, seeking counsel for real-life dilemmas—parents rejecting a boyfriend, the challenge of balancing a career with engagement, or whether to tolerate a husband's vices. The public nature of these questions and answers gave individuals a sense that romantic problems were shared, not isolated. This communal airing of personal issues subtly shifted norms, normalizing conversations about emotional fulfillment within marriage and even acknowledging extramarital temptations.

6. THE IMPACT OF WORLD WAR I ON LOVE AND MARRIAGE

6.1 Separation, Loss, and Swift Engagements

When World War I broke out in 1914, millions of men across Europe (and later the U.S.) were conscripted. Soldiers often hurried to marry sweethearts before shipping out, driven by uncertainty and the desire to secure emotional commitments. War brides hoped for their husbands' return, writing letters that kept romance alive amid the horrors of trench warfare. The mass separation of couples gave urgency to love, with engagements sometimes formed abruptly—some sweethearts had barely known each other.

Casualties and amputations shattered many families. Widows, fiancées who lost partners, and veterans coping with trauma faced a changed emotional landscape. Love acquired a poignancy: it could be cut short by fate, intensifying the sense that one should seize happiness while possible. Women who took on roles in factories or nursing discovered new independence, sometimes returning to peacetime unwilling to settle for old submissive roles in courtship.

6.2 Post-War Shifts and Lost Illusions

After the war ended in 1918, the so-called "Lost Generation" emerged—young adults disillusioned by the conflict's brutality. Writers like **Ernest Hemingway** and **F. Scott Fitzgerald** captured the cynicism and yearning for meaning in post-war novels. Some turned to hedonistic pursuits, fueling the "Roaring

Twenties" atmosphere of jazz, nightlife, and flappers in the U.S. and Europe. Though this is slightly later than the scope of "early 20th century," the seeds were sown in the immediate post-war confusion.

The intense camaraderie among soldiers, the heartbreak of war casualties, and shifting gender norms all impacted how individuals thought about marriage. Divorce rates in some countries rose slightly as spouses realized that wartime changes had estranged them. For younger men and women forging new relationships, the war's devastation made them either yearn for security and familial stability or embrace short-lived romantic thrills. In both cases, the old Victorian ethos of measured courtship lost ground to more emotionally spontaneous or modern attitudes.

7. INTERNATIONAL VARIATIONS AND CROSS-CULTURAL EXCHANGES

7.1 Love in Non-European Contexts

While Western Europe and North America dominated the discourse on modern love, many parts of the world experienced the early 20th century with different dynamics. In Japan, for instance, the **Taishō period** (1912–1926) saw the rise of "modern girls" (moga) who challenged traditional norms by adopting Western fashions and seeking more autonomy in romance. Yet arranged marriages remained common. Similarly, in parts of India under British rule, social reformers debated child marriage, widow remarriage, and women's education—questions tied to how love and marital choice might evolve.

Global travel and communication brought some cross-cultural exchanges. Intellectuals in colonized nations read Western literature, adopting or adapting Romantic and modern perspectives on love. Conversely, Westerners fascinated by Eastern cultures sometimes romanticized "exotic" forms of intimacy, echoing earlier colonial stereotypes. Genuine intercultural romances existed but faced barriers of race, religion, and empire. Overall, the early 20th century was a period of ferment worldwide, but colonial power imbalances and local traditions meant that change came unevenly.

7.2 Influence of Migrant Communities in the West

Large-scale immigration from Eastern and Southern Europe to the U.S., and from rural areas to industrial centers in Western Europe, created multicultural urban neighborhoods. Different ethnic groups brought their courtship customs—some more conservative than mainstream Western patterns, others more flexible. In enclaves like New York's Lower East Side, Italian families enforced traditions on daughters, while Jewish families balanced Talmudic or Old World customs with the new American environment.

Romantic choices in these settings could be fraught: a young woman working at a garment factory might secretly date a man outside her ethnicity or religion. Tensions arose between older relatives wanting arranged or at least community-approved matches and younger people exposed to the "American way" of dating. Love thus became a site of generational and cultural negotiation. Such complexities foreshadowed the melting pot or mosaic approach to love in pluralistic societies.

8. LITERARY AND ARTISTIC EXPRESSIONS: TRANSITION TO MODERNISM

8.1 Strains of Early Modernism

While Romantic influences lingered, a shift toward **Modernism** in literature and art was underway before World War I. Authors like **Joseph Conrad**, **James Joyce**, and **Virginia Woolf** experimented with narrative structure, often focusing on the inner consciousness. Love appeared in these works as a nuanced psychological process, shaped by memory, identity, and social constraints. The flamboyant gestures of Romantic heroes gave way to introspection, ambiguity, and existential questioning.

D.H. Lawrence in England openly confronted sexual desire and the clash between individual passion and societal mores. Novels like *Sons and Lovers* (1913) and *The Rainbow* (1915) portrayed characters who struggled to integrate physical and emotional intimacy with a changing moral environment. Such works were controversial, sometimes banned for explicitness, but they pushed the boundaries of how love and desire were represented, anticipating a broader sexual revolution that would gradually unfold.

8.2 The Visual Arts and Love Themes

Visual arts reflected the transition from Impressionism and Post-Impressionism to Cubism, Fauvism, and Expressionism. Painters such as **Pablo Picasso** or **Henri Matisse** occasionally tackled themes of love and human figures in fragmented or boldly colored forms, emphasizing emotional resonance over realistic depiction. While not all pieces were explicitly about romance, the breakdown of traditional perspective paralleled the breakdown of rigid courtship forms. The idea that love might be multifaceted, subjective, and open to fresh interpretation harmonized with modernist aesthetics.

In parallel, photography advanced, capturing more candid images of couples or family life. Studios offered formal portraits, but the spontaneity of snapshot photography, albeit still limited by bulky cameras, gave glimpses of genuine affection or playful intimacy. Over time, these photographic records would further normalize less staged expressions of love.

9. RELIGION, MORALITY, AND THE STATE

9.1 Ongoing Church Influence

Churches—Catholic, Protestant, Orthodox—retained considerable authority over marriage in many regions. Priests and pastors guided premarital counseling, insisted on public vows, and often discouraged divorce. This moral structure persisted, though younger generations started to see church authority as optional in some urban circles. In Catholic countries, couples who wanted a civil marriage had to follow church guidelines or face social ostracism, reflecting how the old order still shaped love's formalities.

Even so, some clergy recognized that changes were inevitable. Pastoral writings about conjugal life sometimes incorporated the language of mutual support and partnership, acknowledging modern ideas without fully endorsing them. The tension between religious tradition and the new psychological or feminist discourses created a patchwork of practices: in certain parishes, a progressive priest might discreetly support couples seeking a more equitable union, while in another, a strict pastor might condemn any deviation from traditional roles.

9.2 State Bureaucracies and Marriage Laws

Governments continued to systematize marriage records and vital statistics. Some countries reformed inheritance or property laws to offer limited rights to wives, reflecting the partial success of feminist campaigning. Debate around child labor, housing conditions, and public health sometimes intersected with family policy, implying that stable, affectionate marriages produced better outcomes for society. Still, the idea of "companionate marriage" as a legally recognized partnership of equals was not yet entrenched—most laws favored men's authority in finances and child custody.

In the United States, some states relaxed divorce laws slightly, acknowledging marital breakdowns due to cruelty or desertion. Yet social stigma clung to divorced women, who often struggled to remarry or find acceptance. The trend toward more lenient divorce pointed to a future where love might be considered a private affair subject to revaluation if it ceased. Critics feared moral decay, while proponents argued that forcing unhappy couples to remain together was more harmful.

CONCLUSION

In the early 20th century, love was at a crossroads. Vestiges of Victorian decorum persisted, urging modesty, moral uprightness, and parental oversight of marriage. Meanwhile, the nascent modern world introduced psychological insights, urban anonymity, women's emancipation, and mass culture that encouraged freer, more personal expressions of affection. War upheavals, economic changes, and intellectual ferment accelerated the questioning of old norms.

Couples increasingly believed that love should be the core reason for marriage, not just economic security or social standing. Yet legal inequalities, rigid morality, and social pressure still hemmed in many relationships. Innovations in dating, communication, and entertainment provided pockets of liberty, while feminist discourse and psychoanalysis offered new conceptual frameworks. These forces set the stage for the dramatic transformations that would unfold as the 20th century progressed.

By the mid-century, two world wars, ongoing feminist struggles, and the rise of popular media would thoroughly reshape the landscape of love. Although we have not fully entered the modern era in this chapter, the early 20th century stands as a pivotal transitional phase: a period when individuals wrestled with the tension between inherited tradition and the possibilities of a more flexible, psychologically aware approach to romantic bonds. The resulting evolution in love—both fragile and full of promise—would shape the modern relationships of subsequent generations and continues to inform contemporary discussions about intimacy, freedom, and emotional fulfillment.

www.ingramcontent.com/pod-product-compliance
Lightning Source LLC
LaVergne TN
LVHW012105070526
838202LV00056B/5627